Channeling

Roxanne McGuire

Channeling - the psychic awareness of mediums, gurus, seers, shamans, and so on - aims to develop the sixth sense, increase sensitivity and awareness to more subtle levels of consciousness, expose us to cosmic consciousness, develop spirituality and enlightenment via extrasensory guides, enhance creativity, and harness inspiration.

In this book, Roxanne McGuire, a spiritual counselor who practices channeling, elaborates upon this art and provides exercises for developing the channeling ability in people who seek to increase their intuition and creativity.

ASTROLOG COMPLETE GUIDES SERIES

The Complete Guide to Coffee Grounds and Tea Leaf Reading
Sara Zed

The Complete Guide to Palmistry
Batia Shorek

The Complete Guide to Tarot Reading
Hali Morag

Crystals - Types, Use and Meaning
Connie Islin

The Dictionary of Dreams
Eili Goldberg

Meditation: The Journey to Your Inner World
Eidan Or

Playing Cards: Predicting Your Future
Hali Morag

Day-by-Day Numerology
Lia Robin

Using Astrology to Choose Your Partner
Amanda Starr

The I Ching
Nizan Weisman

Pendulums
Jared O'Keefe

Channeling
Roxanne McGuire

What Moles Tell You About Yourself
Pietro Santini

Secrets of the Body: Your Character and Future Revealed
Jocelyne Cooke

Secrets of the Face: Your Character and Future Revealed
Jocelyne Cooke

Astrology
Amanda Starr

Day-by-Day Wicca
Tabatha Jennings

CHANNELING

Roxanne McGuire

Astrolog Publishing House

P.O. Box 1123, Hod Hasharon 45111, Israel

Tel: 972-9-7412044

Fax: 972-9-7442714

E-Mail: info@astrolog.co.il

Astrolog Web Site: www.astrolog.co.il

ISBN 965-494-095-7

Published by Astrolog Publishing House 2000

Printed in Israel

10 9 8 7 6 5 4 3 2 1

Contents

Introduction 7

The History of Channeling 23

Preparing for Channeling 26

The Nature of Channeling 33

The Basic Tools for Channeling 35

Preparatory Exercises for Channeling 37

Soul, Energies, and Chakras 50

The Aura 62

The Use of Meditation in Channeling 77

Performing Channeling 92

Channeling 99

The Influences of Channeling 115

Transition to Cosmic Channeling 137

Channeling via Dreams 141

Channeling Using Crystals 150

Conclusion 155

Introduction

The modern age has provided scientific answers to many questions that were unanswerable for thousands of years. While it is an age in which man has walked on the moon, medications have been discovered for most of the existing diseases, and human achievement has soared immeasurably, there are still puzzles that the human brain has been unable to solve. Among others, the question of our existence in the universe has always been and still is a mystery.

In this materialistic age, we are still seeking for the "truth." People search for answers and for guidance along their paths in life, and since the existing answers provided by religion and tradition do not satisfy them - because generally speaking these answers are not compatible with the reality of the beginning of the millennium - they seek answers from superior forces, from an upper dimension, in order to attain serenity and spiritual calm, and to lead a fuller and more satisfying life.

The typical questions concerning our existence in the world are philosophical or scientific, and they express our desire to know the *reason* for our existence in the world rather than the *nature* of this existence. Moreover, we know that the very experience of the present in the world at any given moment is in fact the answer to all the "existential" questions.

The answers to these questions are not far away. They can be found in every individual. We just have to discover them.

While each one of us wants to believe that there is a higher, hidden meaning to life, which can be obtained by a difficult, protracted struggle, and most of us tend to judge our value according to the standards that we aim to achieve, the truth is that the very fact of our existence on earth is proof of our value. The real challenge is to recognize this, and by means of cognizant consciousness, to understand the meaning of our existence in the world.

Inside every person is his private "inner I"; he just needs to find it. This "inner I" is in constant touch with his reality, is expressed unconsciously, and activates the person intuitively. These intuitions are positive, and improve the person's functioning, but their contribution is enhanced when the person raises them to a conscious level, is familiar with their workings, and navigates his life accordingly, following improved and more qualitative criteria.

Nowadays, the process of raising this intuitive sensitivity to an everyday conscious level and to the awareness that activates the person is called "channeling."

The word "channeling" means creating pipelines of contact and communication. This basically describes the entire concept.

Channeling is an extremely simple concept, and it means the conscious raising of the inner nature, the inner consciousness, the inner spirit, to cognizant consciousness. This inner consciousness is infinite, and is unlimited in terms of time or space, so that the examination of the individual's nature can gain momentum, and attain a full recognition of consciousness on a cosmic background of past and future, far beyond what the regular human eye can discern. Furthermore, by means of channeling, the channeler can raise other people's "inner I," and in this case, he serves as a voice for others, and can reach the general, absolute, infinite reservoir of inner consciousness.

In scientific terms, it is possible to say that channeling is the contact that is created and that causes a passage of energies between the various layers in the body or the universe, that is, the combination of the physical and spiritual energies of individuals by means of accessibility to realms that are inaccessible in daily life, and linking them to the spiritual energies of the entire universe. Thus, the term "channeling" also means openness to love, to energies, and to conscious contacts with large and lofty dimensions of existence.

Channeling is in fact a tool that is used in different ways, although people are not always aware of its use.

Channeling effects a change in the personality of the channeler, and brings about a different view of the nature of man in the cosmic whole. This conclusion is a result of the analysis of the experience of channeling.

However, it is first necessary to understand the nature of man, his place in the universe, and the factors that constitute his body and soul, and only afterward to understand the contribution of channeling to the improvement of the individual and of society in general.

We will avail ourselves of psychological theories (mainly Freudian and Jungian). If we relate to the person's soul as the factor that influences his thoughts, desires, and deeds, we see that the soul comprises three spiritual structures: the conscious, the subconscious, and the unconscious.

The **conscious** is the spiritual structure where the feelings the person is aware of at any given moment are located. For example, at this moment, the reader is conscious of the text he is reading. Or toward lunch-time, the person becomes vaguely aware of the hunger that is beginning to bother him.

The **subconscious**, which is also called the "accessible memory," includes those experiences that are not conscious at that particular time, but are easily retrievable, either spontaneously or with minimal effort; for example, the memory of a favorite dish, or of what one did today or yesterday.

The **unconscious**, which is the vast, profound layer of the human soul. This is a structure of innate impulses and instincts, emotions and memories, as well as of gradually repressed urges such as traumas, latent emotions, sexual desires, and so on, which were pushed unconsciously into the unconscious soul.

The three layers have a profound significance in human functioning, but the unconscious layer, even though it is barely known, is the one that influences people more than anything else, because the really important aspects of human functioning are molded and directed by impulses that are outside of the conscious realm. Factors of which a person is unaware can be disguised and can influence him in the form of instinctive impulses that manifest themselves indirectly in dreams, in unconscious behavior, in intuition, and so on.

In effect, this is the deepening of the understanding of the nature of the link between the conscious and the unconscious, and between the outer environment and the inner one, and the compatibility of these elements, which are sometimes contradictory, when they are reflected in each other.

Self-awareness distinguishes the individual by means of the "brain," relying on the reflection that is radiated outward

Instinctive impulses

to the physical world. If it were possible to imagine looking at the world from the outside, and not through the eyes of the observer, it would be possible to notice that the person is the meeting point in which objective reality turns into subjective actuality. This is in fact a process that creates a direct link with our existence. The mind, the subconscious, and the unconscious always accompany us, and are within us.

The revelation of the power of love, as an expression of the spiritual connection, is a significant characteristic in understanding channeling, as is the participation of the individual in helping and supporting others, which is what causes awareness to broaden beyond private concerns to an awareness of universal cooperation, raising human consciousness to higher levels.

Some people define the unconscious universe as man's reservoir of spirituality, and channeling as the experience of creating a communication pipeline to the highest inner sphere of the unconscious.

It is impossible to define the mind scientifically. It is similar to the personification of the divine nature. Only the existence of spirituality in the human soul can be defined. Generally speaking, it is claimed that all human beings are blessed with a certain degree of spirituality, and are part of a spiritual, self, and high existence. While human beings are not God, there is something of the divine awareness in their souls.

As individuals, we safeguard the individuality that is within us, but during channeling, it broadens from the point of view of spiritual understanding to the stage of understanding all the individual details at the level of "general I," a stage that is nearer to the divine stage.

As part of the infinite divine being, human beings are also part of an infinite being. Man's birth and death are part of a

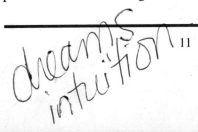

bigger, eternal system that can only be understood via a deep inner vision.

Every person is tied to his superior existence, although he is unaware of this; this knowledge is located in the subconscious of his inner being.

Channeling with the subconscious, and bringing it to the conscious level, can be done by learning, which causes the person to become familiar with the experience of discerning the truth and touching the high energies that are in his character. This is also the path to an encounter with the general truth and the upper spheres that are common to all human beings and to the whole universe.

The beginning of channeling is in fact in the journey of self-discovery that penetrates the person's *inner being* and brings him closer to *his truth*, to the upper and inner spheres *in him*, or, if you like, to the unconscious that is *inside him*.

The journey to self-opening can occur at any moment and without prior preparation. It is sometimes difficult to pinpoint the particular moment at which the true revelation takes place, but it is easier to discern its results.

The result can be expressed in poetry, writing, dance or any kind of action, but there can also be a complete lack of physical action; it can be the development of the awareness of understanding into the inner being that is hidden from the person's reality. An encounter with this reality will lead to release and to seeing the truth in broader perspective.

When people engage in meditation, which also serves as a means of channeling, it is possible to feel the self-energy and love that flow in the inner part of the body, even though in this case there is no verbal expression of them. This is the channeling that is comprehensible to almost everyone.

The process can be explained when we examine our

reaction upon meeting a stranger. During the first encounter, we create in our imagination a characterization and a visual memory of the person, which we use during our next meeting with him.

During meditation, we concentrate on that same visual memory of the person, penetrating the "inner view" of the image - the one that was not absorbed by the eye during the encounter, but rather by the subconscious. This penetration goes into the mind, into the energetic fields, and into the "inner I."

Most people channel with their inner self, which is located at a higher level than the "external self," or with the subconscious that is within them.

Some of them channel by means of dreams, or by means of a sudden inundation of spirituality; others channel during artistic creation; and still others enter this state by listening to music.

Spiritual awakening is not the preserve of the "chosen ones" only. The concept of chosen ones is obsolete. Every person is, in effect, "chosen," and the proof of that is the fact of his physical existence in the world. Every person chose and was chosen to come into the world. However, not every person experiences the truth, his inner being, or the encounter of the conscious with the unconscious that is in him; or perhaps he experiences them without a clear awareness of it, but this does not mean that he is incapable of this encounter. What generally separates the person from his inner truth are the factors that cause him to flee from coming to grips with reality. For example, religion (in its blind and extreme form of "foolishly pious") and drugs help people escape from the struggle with reality, and prevent them from coping with pain and its consequences by leading them into

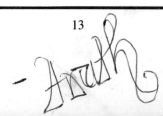

"another world." Not for nothing is religion often labeled "the opiate of the masses." Religion controls the person - as do the government, the authorities, etc. An obedient citizen is a good citizen, but he is not necessarily a person who is aware of his inner character.

This "game" has to change. Obedience is a positive factor, since every democracy, no matter how liberal, has to be based on a conscious awareness of its advantages, with every person's inner criticism of its failures and drawbacks. This is how the individual's thinking about himself should be. It would be good for every person to search deep in the recesses of his soul for the truth, his private "I." The person can give himself everything he can possibly desire, and only he can avoid what he wants to avoid. Channeling will expose these desires, and if the person is able to channel, he will control the processes that will beset him as a result of this exposure without resorting to drugs or fake religion as a refuge. He will realize his true nature in this world, since the energies necessary for action in every field of life are hidden inside him.

Reward is not in heaven, either. Reward is in this life - it just has to be discovered, and not denied.

It is very difficult to eradicate a concept that was planted in us at birth - about the next world and paradise - but the result of the channeling experience helps us understand that there is no reward except for the one that is provided at this very moment, and there is no external paradise beyond the place where we are now. When the person's inner consciousness recognizes the existence of these facts, it will uncover the universal dimension of the universe. All the erroneous perceptions that man has grown up on for thousands of years have to dissipate during channeling.

There is no way of negating them other than recognizing them as "diseased" elements that requires healing, and it must be remembered that the positive perceptions, that is, the positive energies, are the ones that help, because they constitute positive messages for the channeler.

The most basic and fundamental channeling is the kind that enables the person to accept his character at any given moment. The body, mind, and spirit are supposed to guide him as to where to place his positive energies, such as love, compassion, helping others, and so on, so that the reasons for his living in this world can be understood, as can the significance of his existence here and now.

Since all the inhabitants of the cosmos are constantly in a permanent state of growth and change, our characters also require broadening and development, in order to keep up with the pace of life's change and growth. The purpose of the "tools" with which channeling provides us is to answer the demands of the individual for a broad, aware and in-depth understanding of himself as a part of the cosmos.

The people who are open to the new awareness that they encounter during the process will gain more profound wisdom and love, by means of which they will be able to "discover and accept" themselves in broader proportions. In this way, they will contribute to the essence of life itself and influence it, since they will be able to touch and improve with "the general responsibility" of the universe that we share by our very existence in it.

The first step in this journey is to reach the understanding that the world operates for us, and not against us. When the person is not satisfied with his life, when he suffers, or when he feels deprived (even if objectively this is not the case), he goes out in the most natural way and fights to improve his situation. The more fiercely he resists and fights, the longer the present situation will persist, and the deeper the struggle against him will be, until all the negative feelings become permanent features that ultimately work against him. By means of channeling, it is desirable and possible to reach the understanding that life as it is, is in fact the positive and creative part of the world, while struggles, fights, and resistance are the root of evil.

The only thing that is necessary is to recognize the fact that the person is what he is, and his existence in the world here and now is the correct, true consciousness. After all the searches for and theories pertaining to a better world or a better life, the acknowledgment of life in this world, and the pleasures of the moment from simple and natural things, is the whole theory in a nutshell.

People spend their whole lives investing their best efforts in becoming someone else. They construct a set of expectations for true self-realization, sometimes consciously, and sometimes unconsciously, but all their actions are aimed at realizing these expectations. The truth, which is manifested in channeling, reveals the simplest thing, but the hardest to understand intellectually: every person, by being a person, is the real thing.

If people devoted a few minutes to thinking about that, they would understand that accepting this theory is not so simple, because the individual desires and the human mind are controlled by the erroneous certainty of the wish to be someone or something else. Only by being the people they really are can they experience the true and positive feelings of love, freedom, joy, and so on.

In the same spirit, we have to ask if the possibility of choice that we have been given is the result of convenience, of aspirations, or of self-completion, and what obligations we stipulated for ourselves and for others.

The person's basic obligation is, by nature, toward himself. When it does not clash with that of the good of other people, there is no problem. But in most cases, the person's wishes and self-obligations encounter those of other people who do not always see eye to eye with him, and this is where the conflict occurs, as a result of which there is liable to be discord. In order to solve this conflict, a broader and more comprehensive view is necessary, which will enable our thoughts and emotions to be transformed into the understanding of the individual's nature within the total fabric of society, as a continuum that completes everything and works toward improving the nature of society as a whole

If we are sick with some disease, we listen to our bodies and to the messages it transmits to us about the disease, and we adopt the appropriate healing method accordingly. The identical treatment for the spirit and mind will also effect a speedy recovery. When the spirit and mind are injured and do not respond, the body is the one that is injured, so they should be heeded, because both the spirit and the mind send messages. We must examine ourselves, select the positive messages, such as self-love that should be nurtured, and also the rest of the positive energies - not to harm others, not to patronize others or be proud - and dictate reality according to the values of those energies. This awareness will prevent a situation of imposing restrictive laws, since a person with positive conscious awareness has no need to impose such laws, when love is the dominant law.

This is in fact an objective with a supreme purpose, toward the accomplishment of which every person, in his own little world, can contribute. As we said, the realization can be expressed in words, in revelations, in art, and so on.

Everyone channels in his own way; no way is better or worse than another. Every way that realizes the inner energies in every person is the best way for *that person*.

Many people latch onto the subject of channeling as a result of their innate curiosity that motivates them to seek what is hidden behind unexplained phenomena. This trend must not be scoffed at, as long as it does not contain any negative motives, since the whole essence of the channeling experience stems from the positive energies in the person. But since most people are skeptical by nature, and are not inclined to believe in beings that do not have a physical form, this concept, like all the other mystical concepts, is not easily grasped, and is not accepted with understanding (in contrast to sciences that can be proved in "black and white").

Accordingly, people have to cope with the fear of the unknown, with the anxiety of coming into conflict with abstract elements. There are people who have the ability to perform the procedure by themselves; they have certain properties that enable them to realize this marvelous journey. However, many others need the guidance and direction of an external factor, whose role is to help them along this long journey.

There is no need to fear channeling. The desire to open oneself to a high sphere of self is natural and desirable. However, the person should first open up inwardly, personally, before channeling with external elements.

The strength and power that will be drawn into this experience are what will make channeling with the rest of humanity and with its higher awareness possible. With the help of high inner awareness, it is possible to channel with other forces. Moreover, when channeling with external forces follows the establishment of the connection with high personal inner awareness, it is possible to channel with elements chosen beforehand, and not just incidental ones.

The freedom of choice in external channeling will exist in its best form only when the process is performed after and by means of high personal inner channeling, when the stage is reached in which the experience will be felt in its full power.

Some people channel by means of high personal awareness that is *supported by an external guide*, who helps decipher the messages as clearly as possible. The guide can interpret the experiences in the best way, and translate them into words that are easily understandable, and whose meaning is easy to absorb.

In order to channel and experience the event privately, concentration and profound intention are required. It is important to be aware of the object by means of which we want to channel, and the kinds of action that are needed in channeling.

If we want other people to participate in the meeting, the event should be prepared in every detail before inviting those with whom we want to share the experience.

Not everyone is able to channel with the overall cosmic experiences, since not everyone has a sufficiently high level of channeling properties - but everyone can reach a level of inner personal experience of channeling toward love and toward his inner energy.

Channeling is an action like the rest of the actions that

exist in this world. Most people need a great deal of patience and a lot of practice and persistence in order to perform this action. For those who persevere, and really and truly wish to be uplifted, the action is certainly possible. There is no doubt that channeling is not the preserve of very gifted people only.

The simplistic way of channeling is to sit peacefully and quietly, to concentrate, and to ask in a personal way, or accompanied by a guide, to channel with one's inner self. When the channeling happens, one has to open up and listen very attentively to the thoughts, messages, or words that come up. It is possible only to listen to thoughts, and it is possible to repeat them in words. At a high level of concentration, it is possible to ask the guide to speak from inside the body of the channeler.

The higher the level of channeling, the easier it is for the channeler to open up to the love and wisdom inside him, and to bring them to the conscious reality of his life.

This experience, according to people who have undergone it, bestows a feeling of calm, serenity, lightness, and floating. Time is suspended, the person and his surroundings are shrouded in silence, and a sensation of the strong presence of tremendous energy floods the body and the entire vicinity. The air is flooded with currents of love, warmth and communication, and all one needs to do is absorb the energies that are flowing and flooding.

While the absorption of the external energies is postponed for a later stage, after the first stage of becoming acquainted with the inner self, it is then higher, more spiritual, and something to be aspired to.

The absorption of those energies occurs only after freeing oneself from the bonds of skepticism that surround us, even though the process does not mean repressing doubt, nor

20

wanting to ignore the truth of things. The correct way is to come close to doubt, and not negate it, to cope with the gnawing questions, and to overcome them, either by one's own forces, or accompanied by an external guide.

Every person is capable of taking a journey inside himself. Certain properties are necessary, and they have to be developed in order to perform the process - but it is possible and can be learned.

The first and most important property of all is to remain *stable* throughout the process.

Since our world is built out of a combination of the physical factors that dictate the actions of the universe and the spirituality that populates it, it also has an effect on the private world of every person.

The balance between a person's body and its actions on the one hand and his spirit and his brain on the other must be maintained, and neither of these factors is less important than the other.

This stability will help the person in his channeling journey, during which he leaves his inner being for higher spheres, but he *must return* to his previous state at the end of the journey, without undermining his physical and mental stability.

No activity of this kind must be undertaken without prior preparation, whose role is to stabilize the person and to provide him with suitable tools for the experience that lies ahead.

Only physical and mental stability, and the balance between them, can bring the person closer to the exposure of his inner being and to the truth inside him, and bring him back to his world safe and sound.

We are not talking about crystal balls by means of which it is possible to predict the person's future, nor are we talking about a medium who speaks in the voice of a dead person. This experience is mental and spiritual. It is more abstract, more spiritual, and penetrates more deeply into the person's soul, lifting him up into higher spheres, without the need for external aids.

The channeling journey is an exciting inner movement toward self-awareness. The person becomes acquainted with his inner self, and in this way, the journey grants the traveler a fuller life, a life with a broader dimension, and a basic and deeper understanding of his nature. It broadens and develops the depth of the person's thought and his creativity, and enables him to see beyond the narrow reality of his life, and to blend into the universe, as a part of it.

It causes the person to be positive, pleasant and useful, and develops in him the awareness of helping others.

During the course of this journey, the person is supposed to liberate himself from the forces of evil that are at work in him. Vindictiveness, malice, envy - all these are liable to be detrimental to his overall traits. In contrast, positive forces such as love, self-control, benevolence, humility, and modesty will increase. Jealousy will give way to simplicity and kindness, and envy will be replaced by personal responsibility and love of others.

The History of Channeling

The concept of channeling in its broad sense is not new. The connection with the supernatural is ancient, even though every era presents different channeling journeys and different stages on the path to self-identity.

Man has always searched for answers to his questions, answers that were not "visible to the eye." The main question was always man's existence in the world - his origin and what happens to him after death - and various answers and interpretations were offered throughout human history.

The ancient Egyptians believed in life after death, and their belief was based on the premise that man's "life" accompanies him to the afterlife. They were among the first to postulate that channeling occurs in dreams, and through it, the messages are transmitted to the person's brain.

The ancient Chinese mediums who lived about 10,000 years ago experienced an alien presence, advised the leaders how to act, and transmitted vocal messages from dead people that they heard during visions.

The Children of Israel, who were idol-worshippers before they received the Law from Mount Sinai, committed themselves to the belief in one God - an unseen God. "Thou shalt not make unto thyself any graven image." The concrete expression of divinity changes image, form, and - most importantly - content. God is invisible, and imperceivable. This is a spiritual concept, beyond man's simple comprehension. His intellect must understand and absorb the nature of God. This is the beginning of spiritual abstraction in the consciousness of the human brain.

Abraham was prepared to sacrifice his son, Isaac, after he heard the voice of God commanding him to do so. The prophets - the true prophets - who were actually channeling pipelines between man and God, expressed the theory of truth in their prophecies, as well as the uplifting of the spirit to the highest spheres, and their prophecies (that emanated from a state of trance) were rebukes about the sins of the people, which distanced them from the absolute truth, namely, the correct way of life.

The next world was perceived as a world of justice and truth. Angels wandered about in it, and only the just would get there. The evil would be dragged to hell, and their fate would be bitter. That is to say, there was life after death, and it was an abstract and spiritual life.

The nineteenth century saw a burgeoning of spiritualism, as well as a search for the essence of man's existence and survival in the world. As a result of this tendency, the trend of religious adherence as an outlet for mental problems grew. Wars and loss of human life turned the hurting masses toward seeking answers in spiritual rituals that were performed in churches, and in this way, they found the strength to continue living.

In the twentieth century, there was an increase in the tendency to investigate the supernatural, and in the attempt to channel with spirits that had left the world, as well as the tremendous desire to explore the unconscious in order to live a fuller life.

The modern expression of spiritualism in the New Age is particularly obvious in modern art, in the great creativity in the realm of architecture, in science, in discoveries, and so on.

In any case, this is a journey into the unknown that is inside us, uplifting it to the higher spheres of our selves, just like a journey into the expanses of the universe, which joins all the upper spheres into a superior plane.

Channeling is a process that leads to those spheres.

Since there are no two people whose characteristics are absolutely identical, it is logical to assume that different people will not achieve identical results from channeling. Indeed, every channeler is unique, and reaches a different interpretation of his truth. However, since the highest truth is infinite, and is not dogmatic by nature, it is a general truth, and every person can find what he is seeking in it.

Some people look for a revelation in channeling, and want to invoke an admired and well-known figure such as Cleopatra, Marilyn Monroe, Moses, Jesus, Buddha, Napoleon, and so on, while others want answers to their personal problems, and penetrate into their inner being in order to find the wisdom and the inner nature of their existence, sometimes with the help of a private guide. Every method is correct, as long as it broadens consciousness beyond what it was. This channeling event is ultimately supposed to cause the person experiencing it to have a better and fuller life.

This journey requires maximum caution and attention. It is liable to be dangerous if the person does not prepare for it properly, and there must be full awareness of the process before embarking on it.

Preparing for Channeling

1. Neutralizing negative energies

Energies exist in our bodies and in the entire universe, and they can be exploited for good or for evil. Positive energies are the energies of light, and negative energies are the source of darkness.

Every person has the right to choose between taking the path of positive energies and taking the path of negative energies.

The choice of negative energies is generally a result of negative feelings that dominate the person's personality. For instance, the feeling of jealousy derives from a lack of self-confidence, from guilt feelings, or from an inner need for power.

However, superior justice (which some people interpret as divine power) and reward and punishment are stronger than anything else in the universe, and they are the ones that have the final and decisive control. Despite the fact that humanity has laws that are dictated by the very need to run a healthy society, superior justice sees beyond human justice, whose aim is to punish the guilty. Superior justice is broader, more basic, and sees the reason for things. Therefore, to rise above simplistic perception is the aim and the purpose.

In order to channel, we first have to be in a state of strong self-control so as to neutralize the influence of negative energies. We have to be in full self-control of our physical awareness, in order not to be swept away and harmed during channeling. In addition, we have to be in good health - in our mind, spirit, and emotions, too.

Health problems are liable to cause negative energies to be radiated back at us.

Part of the channeling action is linked to removing subconscious barriers that are liable to be a reminder of various periods in the life of the channeler, which for various reasons were repressed in the subconscious, and only by coming to grips with them can they be solved, thereby permitting the channeling journey to continue. Every stop at this kind of barrier will hinder progress until the barrier is removed.

Jealousy is an example of a barrier, and until we overcome it, we will not be able to proceed on our journey. The barriers of jealousy should be removed by bestowing feelings of warmth, understanding, love, and so on. Jealousy must be fully exposed, and transformed into positive and fulfilling values such as trust and dialog.

By means of removing the barriers of jealousy (not circumventing or repressing it), it is possible to bring the will to change to the conscious level. And this should be the case with every negative energy: we must choose one direction, and direct hatred, fear, jealousy, and all the destructive and negative properties into positive and creative channels, thus bringing about development, realization, and progress.

2. Prayer

Prayer, the source of which is a request for help in some situation of distress, "touches" the layer that is meant to grant the request. This layer also contains negative energies. When prayer is performed with greater intention and devoutness, it neutralizes the negative influences. Thus, the fulfillment of the worshipper's request is in fact dictated by the very uttering of the request, that is, the worshipper is the one who determines the extent of the beneficence and help that he will be granted.

3. Colors

Colors are likely to protect the user against injury during channeling, since the use of the cover of colors protects against negative influences.

White, gold, and blue are the most positive. White symbolizes purity and impeccability, blue symbolizes femininity and links up with love and maternal feelings, and gold symbolizes the sun and the light, and attests to spiritual energy, which can neutralize negative elements.

4. Symbols

Symbols can influence moods, serve as calming elements, and even cause fears. They also help people concentrate and focus on a particular subject.

First of all, we have to learn how to build symbols.

The three basic symbols are:

From these basic symbols, other symbols can be "created." It is desirable to choose a personal symbol according to personal feeling, although the symbols are based on pre-defined aspects.

Star of David (also known as "Solomon's Seal") - symbolizes the joining of the conscious to the subconscious, and attests to the harmonious balance in nature, but also to the struggle between the forces of light and darkness.

Center of infinity - a symbol that helps in centering.

A cross inside a ball - a very powerful symbol, which symbolizes the four elements: air, earth, fire, and water. A very influential symbol in Christianity. It is recommended to focus on the center of the cross as if on a golden, multidimensional sphere. This symbol also helps to get rid of negative energies.

Triangle - a symbol of security.

Five-pointed star - symbolizes touching upper spheres. The pentagram developed from this star.

In addition, the *ankh* can be mentioned, symbolizing the triumph of the spirit over the material, and the *yin* and the *yang*, ancient Chinese symbols that indicated the flow of masculine and feminine energy.

Preparatory Exercises

The preparatory exercises for channeling are done with the help of a partner, when one of the pair is the protector and the other is the protected person. It is preferable for the first "protector" to have experience in channeling, but it is not necessary.

Exercise 1
The partners should sit opposite each other, and should both be expansive, calm, and centered, so that the protector can imagine an aura around the protected person.

By means of using one of the protective colors (white, blue, or gold), the protector must imagine the radiation of color onto the protected person for about 15 seconds.

Stop.

Repeat the action with the next color.

Stop.

Repeat the action with the third color.

Stop.

Speak to the partner about the experience and about the influence of the various colors.

Switch roles and repeat the exercise.

Exercise 2
Repeat exercise 1, this time using a symbol or several symbols. That is, radiate a symbol onto the partner.

Exercise 3

The partners should sit opposite each other, and should both be expansive, calm, and centered.

Imagine radiating a color, a symbol, or any abstract concept onto the partner for about 15 seconds.

The protected person must imagine returning the radiation to the protector. While doing this, the protected person is passive, but feels the protector's action. This exercise does not succeed easily, and must sometimes be repeated after a short rest in order to feel the radiation that links the two.

Stop and return to terrestrial reality.

Switch roles and repeat the exercise.

The Nature of Channeling

In contrast to most of our natural abilities, which can be examined with the help of one of our physical senses, channeling cannot be examined in a concrete way. Despite this, it is innate in us, although not to a fixed extent. There are people with a rich layer of this dimension, and others with less - but every single one of us has it. It is necessary to discover it; it can be developed, and its influence increased.

The penetration into the mysteries of the subconscious broaden the person's horizons, and give him a true and correct perspective of those things that cannot be seen, or cannot be grasped by means of the five senses by which we can define everything around us. It broadens the depth of thought and inspires our creativity, so that we can look at ourselves from the side, and, as a result, appreciate our existence in a more real and complete way.

Channeling is a process of a person entering himself, or, in other words, penetrating his subconscious, and raising it to the conscious level.

As a result of this penetration, self-sensitivity will go up a rung, and its results will make their mark on our activities in various areas of life. A painter can animate the figures he paints, and architect will design the building he is working on more professionally, and so on. Creativity in every field we engage in will acquire dimensions of depth, and will breathe life and power into our every deed.

The penetration into the subconscious, and the "drawing out" of the subconscious into the conscious realm is one facet of the channeling experience. But channeling has another facet, which is characterized in spiritual types. The latter increase the extent of the power of spirit inside them, and "go up a sphere" to dimensions of high spirituality, at a level that can channel with elements that are outside of the inner being of the person himself.

Whatever the case, this journey must be undertaken with extreme caution, very precisely, and only after the appropriate training has been given, in order not to be dragged down into mental problems or a lack of mental stability after the experience has ended. Just like a person should not go into deep and stormy water without learning to swim, he should not try spiritual experiences without prior training. Otherwise he could be swept away, and drown.

It is important to point out that one must discern the fine border between channeling and self-delusion, since at the beginning of this journey, among other things, the feeling of strength and power increases, accompanied by the feeling of mission, which causes a *feeling* of knowing the absolute truth, differentiating between good and evil, and knowing justice. These feelings, which are not necessarily correct, are liable to deceive the person experiencing them, and, furthermore, cause him to deceive others.

True consciousness is still not the preserve of many - only of a privileged few, who link up to universal truth.

To this end, we can examine the biblical prophets. The true prophets are those who saw the Divine Revelation, and their words were received from heaven, as a result of a direct and true connection with God, while the false prophets posed as God's spokesmen, erred, and deceived the people, even though they were sometimes naively convinced that they were true prophets.

The Basic Tools for Channeling

As we mentioned previously, channeling requires suitable training. Part of this training is done by the person himself, as a preface to the actual experience. Only after this training has been internalized can he go on to the next stage.

It is important to remember that the key to the success of the process lies in the knowledge that it is imperative to stay strictly in control of all the stages, reach maximum balance, and not get swept away in a loss of control.

The body must be in a good state of health, since it has an effect on the behavior of the brain. Similarly, there must not be any "complications" in the mental state.

Remember that the body undergoes certain changes during the experience, but they are completely natural in this event. The energies that operate in our bodies are likely to be stimulated to greater activity, which may accelerate metabolism; the level of adrenaline in the blood rises, and there is a general feeling of tangible physical strengthening, but at the same time, there could also be a vague dulling of the senses. Sometimes there is an increase in sexual sensation.

All these attest to the strengthening of awareness on the way to the inner soul, to the subconscious, or the link-up of the awareness with the consciousness that is located at a higher level than self-awareness.

That is, two types of channeling can be distinguished: the one that penetrates to the inner being, and the one that brings the subconscious to the conscious level.

As we mentioned previously, every person can channel, and with the help of the correct guidance, he will be able to direct the energies inside him to penetrate the unconscious inside him.

First, he has to reach the level where he is able to *see inside himself*. This is a visual experience. The nature of the type of vision should not be discussed, since it is individual. Each person sees different images, colors, and so on. The personal properties of each person are the ones that dictate the picture that will emerge.

The picture does not have to be a concrete vision; it can definitely be a symbolic picture. A concrete event in the person's life can project to various situations that have nothing to do with the picture that caused the vision. The *association* is what caused it.

In addition, channeling has a *vocal significance*, which is expressed in sounds, tones, in a message that is transmitted in words or in an intuitive form. Learning to understand the vocal messages is important in the process of the experience, adds power, and serves as a guideline for the channeler.

Finally, it is important to develop the *feelings* that come to the fore during channeling. A developed sensitivity picks up and discerns feelings and sensations (but also permits full control of the experience itself while it is happening).

The development of the senses in an individual way is the best, since every person is aware of his qualities, and their improvement by means of his own sensations is always the most successful.

Preparatory Exercises for Channeling

These preparatory exercises are meant to deepen the feeling of self-awareness, which is the primary basis for the existence of channeling. The exercises are not difficult; they direct the person toward self-control, a comfortable feeling, and enjoyment of the experience of channeling that will occur later on.

Centering
The body and consciousness must be centered, and at the same time the aura field (to be discussed later) that is radiated by the person and surrounds him must be felt. This action will cause the person to strengthen his aura, to have a high degree of self-control with stability and feet firmly planted on the ground, and will strengthen the person's self-protection.

Exercise 1
The person must focus with concentration on the center of his body (the line of the chakras - to be discussed later) by directing his gaze toward an imaginary shining line that passes along the length of the body. He should try to experience the feeling of light passing along this line; he should avoid any disturbance in concentration during the activity, and should try to experience the peace and quiet around him.

Exercise 2

Do inhaling-exhaling exercises that ascend and descend along the length of the body, and are drawn through the feet into the ground below, and through the crown in the direction of the sky above. This exercise links the person to Mother Earth and to the energies that operate above.

Exercise 3

The person must imagine a focused scrutiny of his image in a mirror or an imaginary lens. The picture that emerges is the observer's individual image, until in the end, his identification with the picture will be maximal (he actually turns into the picture). In this state, the person's balance with himself will be realized; the desired harmony and the centering will be achieved by means of the energies he activated.

This exercise is useful in everyday reality when the person has to cope with a power that is liable to cause a lack of confidence, since by means of centering, the self-confidence of the "weak one" will increase, and he will feel as if staying power and determination are being aroused in him. In effect, he will strengthen the energies in himself - it all depends on his strength of concentration and his inner energies.

Exercise 4

The person has to sit and imagine watching a projector in front of which screens have been placed. On each of the screens the image of the person is projected in a different color, in every color of the rainbow. It is customary to imagine seven screens, with red on the first image and purple on the last. Now the images must be "taken" one after the other, and placed one on top of the other. (The orange image *surrounded by white gold yell, orange white green purp, blue*

must be placed on the red, then the yellow, the orange, the green, the light blue, the blue, and the purple). Each image covers the preceding one perfectly.

The projected color that will be seen in the imagination will be a combination of the colors of the rainbow surrounding by an outline of white light.

The outline of white light is the aura, which contains all the self-awareness. The feeling that will emerge now will be of linking, wholeness, and balance.

Exercise 5
The person must feel as if he is a bottle, and his spirituality as a liquid that is being poured *into him*. When he has the feeling that the liquid has all been poured into the bottle, he must end the exercise.

Exercise 6
The person must dip his hands in cold water and feel the energy of the water rising along his back, and going down his lower limbs until it reaches the ground.

After doing the exercises (all or some), the person must relax and calm down, drink water, and rest, in order to detach himself from the concentration and the effort.

Afterward, he must lift his hands above his head and lower them to the sides of his body, trying to internalize the feeling of pulling into the interior of the body, with a sensation of returning to earth.

Finally, the process must be completed by focusing on the idea of standing in the center of a shining light. This is a symbol of repelling negative energies.

* * *

Channeling exercises play a very important role in everyday life. Besides the calmness and serenity with which they imbue the human spirit, they help each person find his "center" - the stable, calm place that exists in everyone's spirit, from where he can observe the things that happen as a "witness," without getting upset, even if they are irritating or annoying.

Here is the story of Georgia:

Georgia, a 25-year-old senior secretary, and an intelligent and multi-talented young woman, had been born into a very problematic family. During her childhood, she had been subjected to physical and verbal abuse, and had suffered from severe neglect. She had known precious few moments of peace and quiet in her parents' home, since her father, who was an alcoholic in addition to being violent, would beat her mother and the children regularly. At a certain age, Georgia, who was the eldest, began to attempt to protect her five younger siblings from their father, and he rewarded her with endless beatings and curses for her pains.

As a result of the horrendous conditions in which she had grown up, she had learned to survive in any circumstances. From a young age, she had begun to pave her way in life, investing all her energy in her studies, and progressing slowly toward a brighter future.

As soon as she graduated from high school, she left home and began to build a new life. Her progress was meteoric, and she acquired a reputation as a strong, assertive person who was making her way up the ladder of advancement. Wherever she worked, she stood out for her capacity for hard work, her sharp, incisive mind, and her high level of motivation.

After two years in one of the country's largest advertising agencies, she was promoted to senior secretary, serving in fact as office manager, responsible for supervising the work of three other secretaries. Although she had built a new life for herself, with a satisfying social life, many friends, and a wide range of hobbies and interests, Georgia knew deep down that the strong, assertive secretary who always knew what had to be done, how to solve every problem, and how to handle the prickliest clients, was not the real Georgia. She felt that the powerful and seemingly indifferent image she had created for herself was just a facade behind which she concealed her profound fears and extreme insecurity. On the surface, it looked as if Georgia had no problem whatsoever with giving orders, coping with rival secretaries, and letting the whims and the not-always-pleasant comments of her employers roll off her like water off a duck's back. It seemed like nothing got to her; she was always calm and strong.

This couldn't have been farther from the truth, however. The traumas she had suffered in her childhood still dogged her as an adult; they did not give her a minute's peace. Every passing comment that was carelessly directed at her would bother her for hours on end, arouse fears and anxieties in her, and inspire feelings of hatred and anger, even though she was fully aware that the boss had just had another "bad day," nothing more, and there was no need for her to take his comments to heart. Every time she had to criticize one of the other secretaries' work, she would agonize for a long time. Alternatively, she would say what she had to say with a rather aggressive spontaneity that sometimes offended the other woman. As a result, she was under constant stress, and she paid a heavy price in energy and mental strength for every task that was connected to working with people, even though she ultimately accomplished it well. The result was that at the end of a work day, she would come home exhausted and washed out in a way that was completely disproportionate to her actual work.

This situation did not occur only in her workplace, but dominated every aspect of her life. When a guy in a pub or a disco tried to strike up a conversation, she would react with surprising aggressiveness, which was in fact a manifestation of her constant fear of being hurt. She was good at defining her problem: She felt vulnerable, because she was overly sensitive to every word spoken to her, to looks directed at her, to criticism - to the point that she had a hard time functioning after someone in the street or at the bus-stop looked at her curiously. Every person and place seemed threatening and frightening to her, and she expected some kind of blow to strike her at any moment, from an unexpected quarter. She was forced to be forever on the defensive, and worse still, to conceal her predicament with a seemingly "tough" exterior, in order to identify the danger and avert it, and ward off anyone who seemed threatening in her eyes - a role-play that drained her of a great deal of energy.

This behavior pattern occurred with her friends and lovers as well. One inappropriate comment, and Georgia would react aggressively, or break off the relationship forthwith, much to the consternation of the other person, who had not the faintest idea what all the fuss was about.

At her workplace, her superiors' "passing comments"

exhausted her, and sometimes she would come home and burst into tears, turning a comment such as "You should have phoned the client yesterday" over and over in her mind. She felt as if the entire world was against her and wanted her to fail. Because she had experienced profound fears in her childhood, her constant feeling was that she was unprotected, and everything could "get to her" and affect her to the depths of her being. She was in such a bad way that she refrained from going to places where loud or aggressive music was played, or from watching horror movies, because they exerted an extremely significant influence on her mind; after watching such a movie, she couldn't sleep for nights on end. Even on calmer days, she did not fall asleep easily, and her sleep was plagued with nightmares and dreams in which she was being pursued, and managed to escape by the skin of her teeth.

It was recommended that Georgia do exercises one and two when she got up every morning, imagining a line of golden light coming down from up above into the top of her skull (the crown chakra), passing through her spinal column, emerging from the base of her spine, and then penetrating the earth. From there, the light reemerged and entered her body, filled her organs with light, and encompassed her in an elliptical aura of light. In addition, she was advised to inhale the external aura surrounding her, drawing the light into herself, and exhale it back into the aura.

Georgia was rather skeptical to start off with, and found it difficult to believe that it was possible to solve that long-standing, annoying problem that had plagued her all her life. To her great astonishment, the very first times she did the exercises, she reported a surprising improvement.

Suddenly she felt calmer and less agitated. Things that were said in the office, comments and criticism, slid off her without making the profound impression that they used to.

After experiencing the genuine calmness and relaxation caused by these exercises, she asked to learn additional ones. She was advised to do exercise number three - a focused look through a lens or at a mirror - which helps increase one's concentration and energies, as well as letting one see the situation as it is, from a distance, without personal intervention. After Georgia had practiced this exercise, along with the first two, for three weeks, she discovered that it was easy for her to apply exercise number three at work, in the street, or in places of entertainment. When she looked at a person who seemed "threatening" through the lens of the imaginary camera, she felt as if she were not involved in what was going on, nor was she hurt, offended or shocked by the person; she could see things as they were, and, in many cases, understand that there was no basis for her fears about the person. In her workplace, she discovered that she could listen to her superiors' comments calmly, relate to them as constructive criticism, and sift through them without being offended by them.

Anything that was said to her that was irrelevant, or stemmed from a situation of some kind of emotional imbalance in her superiors, washed right off her without provoking any inner reaction. She felt stronger, and far more protected. She found that she had become more tolerant and attentive to the people around her, mainly because she no longer had to examine her feelings ceaselessly, and look for ways to protect herself, and she was able to be more empathetic toward the feelings of others.

She declared that she did not allow a day to pass without doing the exercises at least once a day - and several times on hard days, when she felt more sensitive than usual. Although she felt that spiritually she was not yet ready to get into channeling, she felt that the exercises were promoting her spiritual progress, and once she freed herself of those the difficult moments of "Why did they say that to me? What do they want of me?", she had more time and strength to devote to her spiritual and mental development.

Today, she feels that she lives in a more protected world, since she herself feels more protected, balanced and centered. The feelings that other people are liable to drain her energies from her, or envelop her in negative energies - feelings that were true for her because of the way she perceived them - passed after she learned how to safeguard her energies, and be balanced and centered the whole day long.

* * *

Besides exposing people to higher channels, channeling exercises also help them to ground themselves, that is, to act and function in a better and more balanced way in the practical matters of daily life. This consequence of channeling exercises demonstrates, in fact, that spiritual life and material life in this world are two sides of the same coin, and one cannot exist without the other.

Josh, a young playwright, was a man with many profound mental and spiritual strengths. For many years, he spent his days reading books; he considered creativity and spirituality to be more important than anything else in the world. He spent a lot of time alone, reading books and daydreaming, and even his closest family members considered him a bit of an oddball, and a confirmed recluse.

After graduating from high school, Josh decided that he had to lead an independent life by leaving his parents' home and renting his own apartment. Although he was rather frail by nature, he was certainly capable of working hard - but this possibility did not occur to him. He intended to earn a living by his art alone, and did not take into consideration the obstacles that lay in his path in renting an apartment by himself. He paid the first few months' rent with money that his parents had saved up for him. At the same time, he began to study cinematography in college. Gradually, however, he began to feel that his situation was deteriorating.

Because he was so "cut off" and closed, he did not succeed in leading a lively social life, in exchanging opinions, and in making friends with his fellow students at college. This caused him to lose interest in his studies, and affected his grades and his motivation adversely. He had difficulty sticking to deadlines, was chronically late, and forgot to do essential things. For that matter, he also forgot to pay his telephone, electricity, and gas bills, and suddenly found himself without the above mentioned utilities.

He realized that he had to find himself a job post-haste, but the thought of it frustrated him terribly. If he only could have, he would have spent his days daydreaming and reading books about success, fame, love, and a better future. In actual fact, he didn't do too much to make these dreams come true. Even when he wrote screenplays and plays, he would put them in a drawer, feeling that the process of looking for a place to publish them was too difficult and tiresome for him.

When he finally found work as a salesman for a cellular phone company, he revealed himself to be an extremely unmotivated worker, a daydreamer, a person who forgot instructions and tasks, and was unable to work to schedule.

He soon found himself unemployed again, with his debts accumulating inexorably. He felt powerless. On the one hand, his personality apparently refused to recognize the importance of the material side of life, and on the other, the world slapped him in the face, trying to force him to acknowledge reality. Although he tried with all his might to convince himself to look for a new job, his motivation was non-existent.

He began to feel isolated and lonely, abandoned, and washed out. As a result of his distress, he searched for healing and assistance through spiritual means. Although the thought of being in the company of other people in a meditation and channeling group did not appeal to him in the least - since he always preferred to work alone - he did not have the requisite knowledge, so he decided to join a meditation and channeling group. At the second meeting, the instructor began to teach the participants the channeling exercises. Josh, who was always tired, listless, and weak, felt their beneficial effect on him. After doing the exercises for the first time, he already felt a little more energetic and in a better mood.

After leaving the meeting with a smile on his face, Josh decided to persevere and practice the exercises on a daily basis. The results were immediate. He became more energetic, more grounded, and more earthbound. These things happened gradually, but after only a few weeks, he noticed that he was relating to his studies in a more serious and conscious way, he was less forgetful, he was aware of the bills he had to pay, and he was paying more attention to his physical needs. In the past, out of sheer laziness, he had been able to get by on bread and cheese for days on end - just as long as he didn't have to put down the fascinating book he was reading and go to the store to buy groceries.

He spent less time daydreaming, since he had begun to be aware of reality, and enjoy it. He began to take notice of other people, including his fellow students. He discovered that the moment he showed a bit of interest and willingness to communicate, he had no problem finding interesting friends - both male and female.

The exercises, which helped him become balanced and grounded, caused him to relate to his body respectfully and seriously, and he began to use natural methods to treat the asthma from which he suffered, and to make sure that he swam daily in order to improve his physical condition and health. After some time, he experienced a natural desire to start working. Unlike in the past, he felt that he was beginning to get bored sitting at home, surrounded by four walls, and he felt the urge to meet more people, to be more active, and to earn money.

He found a job delivering newspapers, which, although it was not very well paid, he enjoyed, since he liked getting up early in the morning and riding around the city streets on his scooter, feeling the wind in his face, and all his senses alert and sharp. These factors also contributed to his creativity and improved his writing, because they added new dimensions of consciousness as a result of encountering new people and situations.

He suddenly discovered that the chaos that had been his faithful sidekick, sometimes making his apartment resemble a disaster zone, was beginning to get on his nerves, and he gradually became more organized, neat and clean. His spirit and soul got stronger, as did his body. He felt more ready to face life's difficulties, which he now considered to be interesting challenges. While he never stopped his spiritual work, still practicing his channeling exercises over and over again, and reaching higher peaks of spirituality, his life in the material world also began to follow the path to success.

Soul, Energies, and Chakras

As we mentioned previously, in order to channel safely and effectively, balance and centering or focus must be increased. To this end, it is necessary to become acquainted with several concepts.

Soul

This is the true essence of man's existence. It penetrates the body during birth, and leaves it at death. The body provides it with a physical tool in order to experience the nature of life by means of the senses, the feelings and the mind, which constitute in fact the whole of human consciousness. The soul is the factor that activates the body, and it is expressed by means of the conscious energies.

The conscious energies

It is not possible to quantify the conscious energies in the human body. The very admission that they exist is the decisive fact. The accepted division of the energies in the body is as follows:

Physical energy in a physical body, in which physical awareness is located.

Ethereal energy, which operates on the human mind, is close to the physical body, and helps balance it.

Emotional energy, which links up with both of the previous energies, and is expressed by means of them. This energy acts as a bridge between the physical, intellectual, and celestial layers.

Energy of intellectual awareness, which links up to the feelings.

Intuitive energy. This is where spiritual existence at a high level of understanding and intuitive awareness is focused. (It is expressed in dreams, meditation, and so on.) This is the energy of channeling.

Energy of the soul is the soul's expression of our vocation in this world. It helps us choose our path in life.

The energy of the spirit represents the highest "I," which channels with the upper worlds outside of our bodies.

Chakras

In every human body, there exists a network of nervous systems and sensory organs, which clarify and internalize the outer physical world. In parallel, there is a sensitive system of pipelines and energy centers in the body - chakras - that operates inside us. This system oversees our physical, intellectual, and mental existence.

The existence of man on the earth entails the fulfillment of both physical and mental needs. The chakras are the linking factor with the universe. That is, they are a tool for self-awareness, or, in other words, a tool for internalizing cosmic energies in the physical layer - and vice versa. It is a system that links us to the universe, through which inner thoughts and feelings are radiated outward, and external influences on our inner being penetrate.

The meaning of the word "chakra" is "wheel." The energies flow in it in a spinning movement that resembles a whirlpool. These whirlpools reach the deepest layers of the body, link the different layers, and serve as the linking factor between the person and the beings outside.

The body contains seven chakras, each with its own

properties. These properties are found within us, and although they do not always manifest themselves in our personalities, they exist, and are never totally diminished. If necessary, they operate spontaneously when they have to react. However, they can be roused and stimulated, and their correct operation helps to improve the positive properties in us.

By means of meditation or channeling, it is possible to stimulate the chakras and cause dynamism in the body, an increase in creativity, enhanced self-confidence - and at the same time, develop humility, love, and compassion.

The chakras are as follows:

Crown chakra - links up to the source of our existence and our awareness of the overall universe. Its color is purple. This chakra is the source of the development of human awareness. In the present era, the human brain, which is developed from the intellectual point of view, is working toward absorbing new types of awareness that go beyond superficial consciousness.

Third Eye chakra - is responsible for intuitive perceptions, for internal spirituality, for ideals, and for imagination. It constitutes the last stop before the crown chakra, to the highest self-awareness. Its color is indigo. This chakra is the center of forgiveness and pity, since it has the power to disintegrate reservoirs of anger, hatred, racism, and all the negative factors that block the development of the positive properties of man, and prevent awareness from reaching its objective in the crown chakra.

Throat chakra - is responsible for relationships between people. It helps remove all guilt feelings, and fills our being with feelings of compassion and forgiveness. Cancels the tendency to control others (or to be controlled), and the feeling of superiority (or of a lack of self-confidence). When this chakra receives positive reinforcements, feelings of guilt or jealousy disappear. In addition, this chakra is the one that causes us to feel at one with ourselves on the one hand, and with the society around us on the other. Its color is blue.

Heart chakra - is the location of the ability to love, to take care of others, and to feel compassion. If this center springs into action before the lower chakras, the person can expect health and sexual problems. Its color is green.

This chakra contains the human spirit, and our true character. This spirit is pure, not damaged by any negative factor whatsoever, a kind of "diamond" that is hidden inside us and observes all of our deeds. When we really and truly become acquainted with this source, we begin to be aware of the true inner spirit. On the physical plane, this chakra defends the heart and the lungs, and when it is injured, there is a danger of health problems such as asthma or cardiac disorders.

Solar Plexus chakra - is the center for feelings and nerves. A sensitivity to the influence of drugs and alcohol. Its color is yellow. This chakra gives us a feeling of magnanimity and generosity, as well as feelings of satisfaction. It is also responsible for the sensation of peace and quiet, for removing pressures and tension, and for concentration and listening.

Sex chakra - is the reproductive and sexual center. Its color is orange. This chakra is also responsible for creativity and knowledge, since it links us to the source of inner inspiration, and enables us to enjoy the beauty around us. The knowledge that radiates from this chakra is not just intellectual knowledge - it is also the knowledge of absorbing reality in the most realistic way.

Base chakra - is the center for the human impulse to exist. It is located at the base of the spinal column, and is responsible for activating the energies that are needed for life's activities. Its color is red. It provides honesty and reliability, mental balance, and the power of direction and aim to life. Therefore it is the source of the emotions of happiness and personal satisfaction.

The existential human nature is manifested in the three lower chakras, when they are influenced by the human properties of individualism, acquisitiveness, and emotion. Cosmic awareness tends to raise energies higher to the heart, which is the center of love, affection, compassion, and so on, properties that are common to the whole human race, and their realization is absolute and completely unconditional.

This tendency is becoming real nowadays because of the development of awareness of what is happening in our world.

The three upper chakras - crown, third eye and throat - express the awareness of the soul. In our generation, awareness is opening up in a spiritual direction by means of the intuitive chakras. For that reason, if we increase the influence of these chakras on the conscious awareness, it will be manifested in a more blatantly concrete way.

But it must be remembered that these chakras do not negate the importance of the lower chakras. On the contrary: the lower chakras serve as the reservoir of power and energy for the other centers.

Balancing the chakras

The chakras operate in harmony. If one chakra is harmed, it influences the others. Therefore it is important to stabilize and balance them, and there are special exercises devoted to this end. Applying the exercises to a certain region will also influence the other regions.

Every chakra is linked by the ethereal body to all the layers of the body (physical, mental, and so on): When there is a temporary imbalance as a result, for example, of a sudden fright, the body recovers quickly. However, when the external influence on the body is profound and protracted, its stability is undermined, and the results are liable to be bad, since the chakra that is responsible for that particular region of the body will become unbalanced, which will have an immediate effect on the entire body.

Since the chakras are sensitive to damage, their balance must be restored by means of exercises that are meant for that purpose, and because the chakras are linked to all the body's systems, it means that an upset in one of the systems is liable to upset all the others as well.

Chakra exercises

The general aim of the exercises is to balance the chakras, that is, to develop the feeling of balance and stability in the body. The exercises are performed by means of broadening the awareness and the understanding. The rate of progress is personal, and its aim is balance and relaxation, leading to an increase in the energies in the chakras. (In parallel, the chakras will also strengthen the aura - to be discussed later - and the conscious energies, since the action of the chakras in the body is like the action of connected vessels.) In addition, they serve as a tool during channeling.

Exercise 1

This exercise must be done with the support of a partner.
Lie on a bed or on the floor.
Ask your partner to massage your aura a few centimeters above your body, starting from the head and going down to the feet. This exercise will calm and balance the aura.

Exercise 2

Stand erect, concentrate, breathe deeply.
Raise inner energies from the feet via an imaginary inner line that passes through the chakras in the body to the crown, and take them down both sides of the body to the soles of the feet, so that an energetic circle is formed.

Exercise 3

Stand or sit in total relaxation.
Inhale and exhale slowly at a steady pace and direct the breaths to each chakra in turn (starting from the base). Feel the energies becoming balanced.

Exercise 4

This exercise is meant to ground you and get you to imagine that you are joined to the earth.

Sit on a chair and imagine that the weight of the world is resting on your crown.

Imagine this heaviness descending to the soles of your feet, passing through every chakra in your body, lingering a few seconds in each one, until it reaches the soles of your feet.

* * *

Jason, a young man in his early thirties, had worked as a salesman in one of the do-it-yourself chains since his teens. He had an excellent head for money, and always knew what the market value of a particular product would be at the present time and in the future. His marketing estimates, which he occasionally mentioned with great modesty, and only when one of the managers asked him to do so, greatly impressed his superiors. His organizational talents, his outstanding ability to predict which products would sell better, where each product should be put so as to attract potential customers, and many other excellent qualities that he was blessed with, led to his advancing to the top of the company's ladder, and being offered the job of head marketing executive.

Jason enjoyed his work very much, and knew that the job he was being offered was a fantastic springboard to a high managerial position. He was fully aware of his talents, and immediately accepted the new job. However, his heart was filled with serious misgivings. Even as a salesman, he acknowledged the fact that sometimes it was difficult for him to express himself clearly, and to clarify his position. Worse still, he sometimes felt that the words just refused to leave his mouth. In his childhood, he had been afflicted with a stutter, but it had disappeared over the years.

After taking on the new position, and beginning to work at full steam, he discovered to his great dismay that it was difficult for him to hold his own in negotiations - an ability that was cardinal in his new job. He would suddenly lose his self-confidence, and feel a kind of inferiority and instability when he was faced with an important client or a supplier. When he realized that the client with whom he was conversing was the director of some large company, he felt paralyzed, had a hard time holding his own in the negotiations, and felt as if he was not succeeding in expressing his opinion and stating the terms of the deal.

In addition, numerous creative ideas and revolutionary new theories about marketing raced around his brain, ideas that could well develop and be advantageous to the company where he worked - and of course, make him successful, but he was simply unable to express them, or to describe them clearly to his superiors, and he did not know how to implement them. In the same way, he would "write" wonderful stories in his mind, but they remained trapped there, and he couldn't get them down on paper. He found this situation endlessly frustrating, since he was aware of his abilities. The interesting thing is that together with his problems of expressing himself, Jason suffered from recurring throat infections, bouts of tonsillitis, and thyroid imbalance.

Since he was well aware of his problem, and was acquainted with the chakras - albeit in theory only - he knew that his problem stemmed from an imbalance in the throat chakra. His girlfriend, Meg, who practiced holistic healing, suggested that they practice the exercises for balancing the chakras together. They began with the first exercise. Meg had him lie down on her treatment couch, breathe deeply and concentrate on his breathing, and she began to massage his aura from head to foot. After the treatment, she let him lie peacefully on the couch for a while and enjoy the calming effect of the aura massage on his spirit. Jason felt that the exercise had relaxed him and given him a feeling of confidence. After they had done this exercise several times, he noticed that even at work, the aura massage dispelled some of the inner agitation that was deeply entrenched in him whenever he came into contact with people. He felt stronger and more sure of himself.

Pleased with his progress, he went on to the second exercise by himself: drawing energy upward from his feet along an imaginary line passing through all the chakras to the crown of his head, and sending the energy downward along the sides of his body to the soles of his feet while exhaling. Gradually, after practicing this exercise several times, he began to do all four exercises on a daily basis. A number of times, while he was doing the third exercise, in which the person has to inhale and exhale via the chakras, he was forced to stop because he was racked by an incessant and disturbing cough that caused thick phlegm to rise in his throat. Meg explained to him that that was one of the ways in which the throat chakra freed itself of blockages, and in spite of the difficulty in doing the exercise, he had to persevere until his chakra attained its optimal balance.

And that is what happened; gradually, the cough stopped bothering him while he was doing the exercise. Another thing that happened during the course of his daily practice was that he had far fewer throat infections, and he felt as if his throat had opened up, was clearer, and enabled air to pass through it more easily. His thyroid became more balanced, and the medical exams he underwent every few months showed an enormous improvement in his condition.

However, there were not just physical changes in his life. He began to feel more sure of himself. When he met with the director of a company that wanted to purchase products sold by the company where he worked, he felt that he could present the products more easily, and make his position vis-a-vis purchase and payment conditions perfectly clear. Suddenly, he found it easy to hold his own in any negotiations. The fear that his voice would betray him, that he would stammer or suddenly lack the words with which to express himself, diminished.

Jason experienced a major breakthrough in the creative realm as well. He managed to describe his innovative ideas clearly, and his powers of persuasion increased out of all recognition. Little by little, he began to feel the need to externalize his thoughts, and those same stories that had been buzzing around in his head eventually found their way onto paper. He derived a great deal of satisfaction from the creative side of his personality.

As soon as Jason's throat chakra began to balance itself, many creative blockages were released, his self-confidence with other people increased, and his ability to translate theory into practice, thought to deed, and to express himself confidently, became simple and easy, and manifested itself in all aspects of his life, giving him a lot of satisfaction and joy.

The Aura

The aura is the energy field that surrounds the physical body. Every object and body in the universe - be it plant, animal, or human - has an aura. The human aura is more complicated and complex than that of plants or animals, because of the spiritual component in those fields.

The energy field of the human body contains concentrations of junctions, similar to the branching of a system of cables. These concentrations of junctions are the chakras, which we have already discussed.

Some scientists claim that objects do not exist - they are simply illusions that are created by vibrations that are caused by the speed of energy. What we absorb by means of our senses are very slow vibrations, and the energy vibrates at the same rate. Whatever vibrates on the physical plane is perceived by our eyes as solid and whole substance. Therefore the body does not comprise layers of organic system, but rather the body is a flowing factor, a dynamic, interactive electro-magnetic field. In other words, we are constructed out of energy and space. The energy that makes up the human body is dense, and this is why it can be perceived by the senses of sight and touch. The aura is less dense, which explains why it is difficult to see it with untrained eyes. However, a simple exercise will enable us to sense it clearly. The understanding of the aura as part of an energetic system can help a person understand the nature of his life and the changes he experiences, and how those changes develop.

Moreover, this understanding assists external, internal, and personal balance, as well as understanding other people in a more genuine and profound way. The aura is a kind of human "physical antenna," which stores all the information about everything the person has done in his life, and about everyone he has met on his way. It stores the information, releases it, and permits it to be retrieved when necessary.

Some people estimate that the aura that envelops the human body is two inches thick, reflects the current state of the physical body, and can change in a matter of a few seconds.

Comprehensively, the aura can be seen to play four roles in man's being:

A discerning role - the ability to discern problems or opportunities.

The adaptive property - identifies the factors that influence us, and helps make the required changes, in order to realize our aspirations.

Response to needs - identifies and copes with problems and challenges, as well as with guilt feelings and distress.

Defense roles - helps improve self-defense in the face of hostile elements and injuries, such as illnesses.

The aura reflects the person in his entirety - physical, mental, spiritual body, and so on. It is important to remember this.

The aura is likely to reveal itself in different forms and in different colors: It can appear as a circle that surrounds the body, as a frame without any defined shape, as an arch - in fact, it can appear in any form, according to the individual's traits.

Sensitive people, especially little children, are likely to discern the aura far more easily than people of average sensitivity. For the latter, who lack the natural tendency to "see the aura in depth" with untrained eyes, there are a number of exercises which train them to see the aura with a kind of inner eye.

The aura can appear in a large number of colors, according to the tendency and characteristics of the person, but it is a good idea to point out several typical and significant colors:

Red - a color that attests to strength, a high work capacity, and a great deal of action. An excess of red is not recommended, because our lives are full of active energies, and any exaggeration is detrimental.

Gray - a color that attests to fear and a lack of self-confidence.

Crimson - a color that attests to great sentimentality, emotionality, and nostalgia.

Pink - a soft color that attests to love and affection that are also directed toward other people.

Yellow - the color of the sun, which attests to the broadening of the awareness, and a high absorption of energy that brings the person closer to the essence of creation.

Brown - a color that helps in organizing material life.

Green - a color that attests to stability and balance in the person's life, as well as to inner quiet and tranquillity in life.

It is also the color of the growth and development that take place in the person toward seeing the inner truth.

Indigo blue - a color that attests to calmness and reconciliation, and to clarifying problems and settling them.

Olive green - a color that attests to properties of compassion and sympathy.

Turquoise blue - one of the healing colors, which attests to success and luck, and prevents the approach of negative and harmful elements.

Light blue - a color that symbolizes acceptance of and harmony with the cosmos. It is a color that represents the good, and exists in the soul of every person. It is also a color that symbolizes focus, which is manifested in the close relationship between a person and his fellow man.

Orange - one of the universal healing colors. It represents joy, vitality, happiness, and especially the ability to bring positive elements and energies closer to the person's personal framework of life.

White (light) - this color characterizes the essence of life, and attests to a high level of spirituality.

Purple - a color that attests to purity, to a high presence of spiritual power. It helps when the person wants to make drastic changes in his life, although he should be wary of exaggerated changes that are liable to cause harm.

Black - the color that swallows negative energies (thereby affording an examination of the positive energies without any intrusive and disturbing elements).

The colors can change their shades over the years, according to the quality and nature of the person's development.

The colors are flexible; they change from time to time, as does the shape of the aura, its texture, and the density in which they appear.

Having said that, it is possible to discern a certain basic model that is characteristic of the aura. Women are seen to have an aura with strengthened energy in the upper part of their bodies, while men are characterized by a strengthened aura in the lower part of their bodies. Moreover, it transpires that in people who think about their future, the aura is reinforced with energy in the region of the front of their bodies, while in people who devote their time to memories and nostalgia, the aura is reinforced with energy at the back of their bodies. As a rule, people with an expansive aura are very powerful and have a conspicuous presence.

The aura leaves the physical body at the moment of death, taking with it all the accumulated life experience, as well as the deep emotions that penetrated and influenced the person during his life.

As part of the development of self-awareness, the understanding and control of the aura must be developed. The aura must be reinforced and stabilized in order to develop the essence of self, as well as the required combination of subconscious and conscious, and the need to cope with the negative energies that exist in the body itself and in the surrounding universe, and are liable to exert negative influences on the person.

The aura is an energy field *around* every person, but it is also a field that links all the creatures of the universe. It reflects our mode of thought and our emotions, and protects us against negative elements that operate inside and outside of us.

If the aura is balanced, then we are stable and balanced. If the aura is not balanced, physical and mental problems are liable to arise.

Although everyone's aura is unique and specific, and fixed at any given moment, every person can *absorb* it in a different way. Every revelation of the aura can be seen by the observer. For that reason, that very aura (at a given moment) can have different forms, colors, sounds, and so on, for different aura readers.

In any case, it reflects the energies of its owner, and can reflect his state of health.

In addition, the aura contains the memory of its owner's experiences in life, and for this reason is actually his whole essence. It includes the karma of his previous lives, his present existence, and his future karma, and for that reason, it is more than he is in his life in the here and now.

Since our existence in the physical world is just a part of our overall spiritual existence, which began before our birth, and continues after our death, the aura expresses our full existence, in which our true nature is realized.

Life is a process that takes on a form and discards a form, the reason and the purpose being dictated by its "spirituality."

Job lived a bitter and wretched life fraught with pain and disaster, but not by chance, and not for nothing. Providence, which dictated Job's birth for disaster, is what determined his future (in this world, in the next world, and in the next incarnation). His sticking to the straight path, his coping with crises, were the incarnation of the aura surrounding him.

The revelation (seeing) of the aura is unconscious. The aura is liable to be seen in times of crisis - or in times of sublime happiness. Since it constitutes a tremendous reservoir of energy, its influence is great, and it can be raised to a strong reverberation in the person's mind, which can be accompanied by sounds and tones, colors and powerful feelings.

In order to practice seeing the aura, we must first acknowledge the fact that in our mind there is a field that is called "the sixth sense."

Many times, unconsciously, we have used this sense, when suddenly an "inner voice" prevented us from going to a certain place, or from doing something, because of a feeling that "something bad will happen." This situation arises when we sense a "heavy or negative atmosphere" enveloping us; or when we meet a person for the first time, and although we are positive that we have never met him before, we nevertheless have a feeling of affinity for this person; or when we feel that someone is thinking about us; and so on.

These examples prove that someone is supplying us with information about a situation we cannot see, hear, smell, taste, or touch (that is, use one of our five senses to grasp the situation). However, we sense it, and recognize the fact of its existence.

This is the beginning of the acknowledgment of the intricacy of discerning the sensitivity that allows the human mind to be directed to broader and deeper channels. By means of practice and training, we can learn about the aura potential in us. In order to develop this sense, we have to effect the release of the mind, be focused on its intention to develop this field, and believe in our power to do this.

In this way, our awareness will be opened up to deeper dimensions, and we will be able to reap huge benefits from familiarity with the sixth sense.

Exercises for perceiving the aura

In order to experience the aura, it is a good idea to be assisted by someone else or by a support group, and to do the exercise in an isolated and quiet room with a relaxed atmosphere. Your body must be calm, seated in a chair, back erect, and hands resting palms upward on your knees. Alternatively, you can sit cross-legged or in lotus position on a carpet, palms upward, resting on your knees.

Sit opposite your partner. Relax, breathe deeply and regularly, and concentrate, until there is a feeling of awareness of every part of the body, beginning with the soles of your feet, via each and every part, until you have a feeling of connection with every organ in your body.

After this, do the following exercises:

One of the pair gets up and stands behind his partner. The seated person imagines the aura field that surrounds the upper part of his body.

The standing person rubs his palms together, and when he feels the energy flowing through them, he stretches his arms out to the sides, as if to embrace the seated person's aura. Slowly he moves his palms in the direction of the seated person's head until he receives a sensation of the aura.

Remember: During this exercise, a sensation of pressure is liable to occur around the seated person's head.

Everyone will experience this exercise differently. If the exercise does not succeed first time round, it should be practiced over and over again, since perseverance will ultimately produce the correct sensitivity and the energies required for having the experience. Take note that the standing person feels the *seated person's* aura with his palms, while the seated person feels the aura around the upper part of his body (as if someone is putting a tight sweater on him).

The sensation of the aura may be received in one or more of the following ways:
A feeling of vibration (especially in the palms).
A change in body temperature.
A feeling of a light wind blowing.
Hearing gentle sounds.
Seeing colors or smelling a delicate fragrance (usually accompanied by a sense of touch).

After a brief pause, get up, stand erect, and concentrate on standing solidly on the ground. Switch roles and repeat the exercise.

After doing the first exercise, move on to the second one, which is similar to the first one, but this time, the seated person has to develop feelings of anger inside him. As a result, his aura is liable to change.

(It must be pointed out that different reactions are likely to occur, in accordance with the character of the person who is feeling anger.)

After about three minutes, the standing person must ask the seated one to free himself from the feeling of anger, and he must ascertain that his request was indeed fulfilled, and that the seated person has calmed down (or has "forgiven," in professional jargon).

Here it is important to feeling the *changes* that are occurring in the aura. Switch roles and repeat the exercise.

Finally, both partners must "shake off" the sensation of the aura by rubbing their hands together and rinsing them in cold water, and in order to complete the release of the energies, it is a good idea to stand on the ground and feel it under one's feet, that is, to link up with reality once more.

It is recommended that the sensations that arose during the exercises be written down.

* * *

Here we have the stories of six friends, who decided to do the exercises for realizing the aura together. The first thing they did was find a pleasant room in which they could all sit comfortably. Before doing the exercises, they made sure to air the room out properly, and saw to it that the room was clean and had a pleasant atmosphere, in order to achieve the optimal results. Three of the friends sat next to the eastern wall of the room, leaning on the white wall (many people have found that a white background facilitates seeing the aura), while the other three sat opposite them, at a distance of six or seven paces. They began by relaxing their bodies, ensuring that their sitting position was comfortable and relaxed, and sitting cross-legged with their palms upward on their knees.

After finding a comfortable sitting position (using cushions to sit on or as back supports, as necessary), they began to take deep but relaxed breaths, concentrating consciously on their breathing. Some of the friends began to breathe "into their organs," that is, they began to breathe right into their feet, calves, thighs, buttock muscles, and so on, all the way up, while concentrating on every organ and feeling it relax with the breathing.

Upon completing the relaxation, they each stood up in their own time, when they felt that their bodies were relaxed and their minds free of all thoughts, calm and centered, and stood behind the person opposite.

Now we will concentrate on describing the experiences of two members of the group, Julie and Brandon. Julie stood behind Brandon, and rubbed her hands together for a little while. Little by little, she began to feel that her hands were warming up a bit, as well as experiencing a very slight tickling or tingling sensation. At the same time, Brandon sat down, closed his eyes, and imagined that his head and shoulders were surrounded by an energy field. While he was imagining this, he felt deeply relaxed, his breathing became deeper, and he felt as if he was concentrating intently.

When Julie felt the energy that was flowing in her hands, she went down on her knees behind Brandon, and spread her arms outward, holding her palms in a slightly rounded position, relaxed, parallel to the sides of Brandon's head. Very slowly, she brought her palms closer to the sides of his head. At a distance of about two inches from his head, she felt a kind of gentle vibration in her hands, which emanated from the space between her hands and Brandon's head. The closer she brought her hands, slowly, to his head, the more she felt as if something was pushing against her hands slightly, as if the space between them and Brandon's body was not empty, but rather as if there were some imperceptible substance between them, pushing against her hands. She "played" with this sensation a bit, feeling as if she was pushing and being pushed by this ethereal substance.

At the same time - so he related afterward - Brandon felt a peculiar and not particularly pleasant sensation on both sides of his head. He felt the sensation "inside his head," as if "someone was playing with his brain," as he put it. When Julie intuitively began to move her hands very slowly (it seems as if she had picked up Brandon's sensation!) in an arch-like movement on both sides of his head, Brandon's slight headache ceased and was replaced by a feeling of calm, and a kind of pleasant and quiet humming in his head.

At a certain point, as a result of her intense concentration, Julie shut her eyes. When she described an arch above Brandon's head, she felt as if it were not she who was controlling her motions, but rather that she was simply tracing an existing outline with her hands. When she opened her eyes for a moment, she saw Brandon's aura in front of her. She saw a kind of boundary line around his body, not very wide, and its color was a shimmering light green. She saw the surrounding line just for a few seconds before it disappeared. It must be noted that the line disappeared the moment she attempted to focus her gaze on it and stare at it. When she saw it, she had not looked at it directly, but had glanced at it randomly, without a concentrated eye movement.

After a few minutes, Julie stood up, straightened, and shook her hands a bit, trying to feel the ground under her so that she could ground herself and get back to earth. Brandon got up a few minutes after her. He felt very relaxed, serene, but a bit "shrouded." Each member of the group got up at the appropriate moment. After they had all washed their hands and grounded themselves (some of them jumped around a few times in order to feel the ground strongly beneath their feet), they sat down together, and each person related his or her experiences. Besides Julie, who had seen Brandon's aura, Mike had seen Jarron's aura, but it had been white, indistinct, and broader. In addition, he said, the closer he brought his hands to the sides of Jarron's head, the more he felt a chilly tickling sensation in his hands, which, he felt, came from the space between his hands and Jarron's head. Tracy said that when she focused on the sensations of energy in her hands, she felt them to be exceptionally warm.

Trevor, with whom Tracy had done the exercise, said that he had also felt a strong, pleasant warmth flowing out of Tracy's hands when she brought them close to the sides of his head. He felt that the heat calmed him and relaxed the muscles of his head and face, releasing tension from those areas. After this exercise, all the members of the group felt a little too "spaced out," so they decided to move on to the next exercise and switch partners in about an hour, after they had rested a bit, had drunk some water, and had digested their personal experiences.

The Use of Meditation in Channeling

In a simplistic sense, meditation is the desire to be a witness, to observe and experience the revelation of the human mind, emotions, and body (or aura) *without reacting* to the revealed vision. It is actually an invitation to the person to become acquainted with himself personally, honestly, and truly, with the aim of "making friends" with himself.

Meditation must not be defined in terms of the success or failure of one or other exercise, since the aim is to experience a moment of relaxation from life's crazy rat-race - simply to live the moment.

Meditation is not a skill that has to be acquired - it is an awareness that exists in us, and has to be exposed by means of alertness that comes from calm, that is, by performing the process in which the brain rises above intellectual activity, in order to experience the simplest form of consciousness, and then the awareness opens up to self-awareness.

Meditation exposes and develops the innate creativity in the person's personality, increases the dynamics of his body, improves the "order of his life," regulates the energy in his body, and enhances the effectiveness (and the success) of his everyday life. In addition, meditation also eliminates obstacles and points of tension and fatigue in the body and soul, which relax during the process.

It is possible to discern the influences of meditation on three planes:

On the physical plane - it brings about the relaxation of the body.

On the mental plane - it moderates and calms the troubled brain, and enables it to concentrate on a specific topic/s.

On the soul-spiritual plane - it "charges the batteries" and affords more effective and positive self-action, as well as more positive interaction with other people.

Concentrating deeply on a particular thought can be considered meditation, even if the person is not aware of it. For instance, we say, "We love ...," but when we say that sentence, we do not really feel the essence of love. When we concentrate on the contents of the sentence, and try to experience the genuine feeling that arises from our love of ..., we are actually creating a small-scale meditation which is directed at the fierce feeling of the love that fills us.

In principle, meditation is the relaxation of the brain, its liberation from the surrounding influences and the dictates of the inner ego, and concentration on the inner truth, while detaching ourselves from everyday existence and linking up with a more genuine inner awareness.

Meditation is the factor that links internal reality with external reality; in other words, it is the joining of the unconscious to the conscious. As a result of meditation, awareness broadens (and this enables it to be of use in channeling).

Meditation strengthens the hold on life, but it also leads to new and improved models of thought and behavior, while focusing the brain and the mind on conscious awareness (which in fact is the channeling action).

Meditation may lead to the "inner I," to the conscious energies, and afford awareness and control of the brain, body and the different layers of the nervous system, so that the person can function more efficiently. Meditation is especially effective during times of crisis or difficulties, helping the bodies and brain remain stable, and preventing disorders in the systems. In addition, it helps overcome pain or fears and worries, by means of meditative "discipline" that increases the threshold of pain, and enables the soul to link up with the mind by circumventing the pain.

Types of meditation

Thought-provoking meditation
This meditation is performed with eyes open or shut, while focusing one's thoughts on a particular object, topic, thought, or symbol. It is preferable to choose a topic or concept that can be controlled, such as an event that contains feelings of love, affection, or some kind of positive feeling (a meeting with the person we love, for example).

Receptive meditation
This meditation requires a feeling of serenity and alertness in order to receive the surrounding inspiration, and, similar to the preparations for channeling, here too there must be a high degree of self-control.

If this meditation is performed in natural surroundings, it can lead to a merging of man and nature, and create the feeling that he is an inseparable part of nature.

Creative meditation
This meditation is similar to thought-provoking meditation, except that here it must be broadened and involve feelings. If a certain event is chosen as the object for

Channeling

meditation, the atmosphere involved in it must be added, as must the active feelings, and so on. If this meditation is performed while listening to suitable music, it can broaden the person's heart with feelings, with sounds, and with impressive sensual experiences.

This meditation is easy to do, and the (mental) risk is minuscule.

Meditation by means of personal or public prayer

During public prayer, the power of the worshippers grows, and exerts a greater influence. However, personal prayer also has meditative power, and it leads to a high level of self-concentration.

It must be emphasized once more that meditation is an action that is performed out of strong *self-discipline*, and as such it should be used routinely in life. It is appropriate for everyone.

Meditation is also part of channeling, but only for a certain type of person. It is not meant for people whose power of endurance is not totally in their control, and who tend to be carried away and cross the border between fantasy and reality. People of this type must absolutely not come anyway near this type of channeling meditation. Only people with a high degree of self-control, those whose spiritual strength is great, who tend to pick up spiritual influences in a selective and controlled way - only those can make use of meditation for channeling purposes.

In order to avoid being carried away by emotions and upsetting one's balance, precautionary measures must be taken during meditation:

Beginners who want to experience meditation must not exceed ten minutes at the outset. The early-morning hours are the most favorable time for this activity.

Meditation should be performed about two hours before or after eating.

Meditation topics that are not understood should not be focused on, so as not to undermine mental stability.

No type of meditation that causes the ego to swell, or promises the illogical realization of desires and wishes, should be performed.

The person must always be self-controlled.

Meditation exercises

Exercise 1
This exercise is meant for beginners, and serves as a basis for the next exercises. It is possible to do this exercise with eyes open or shut, but if it is performed with eyes shut, the person must rest and relax for a few minutes *before* doing it.

Find a comfortable position for sitting straight, and rest the palms upward on the knees. Alternatively, sit in a cross-legged or lotus position, with the palms resting upward on the knees. Inhale while pulling in the stomach and tightening the ribs, and take a few deep breaths while letting the stomach out and releasing the ribs.

Repeat the exercise three times.

Relax and breathe at a normal rate, but a bit more deeply.

Exercise 2

This exercise is meant to reinforce the awareness of the body and release tension. (In the main, it is similar to the exercise described for feeling the aura, so we will not repeat all the stages here.)

Remember that another person or a support group should assist the person in this exercise, and that it should be performed in an isolated and quiet room with a comfortable atmosphere.

Exercise 3

The aim of this exercise is to develop the imagination.

Imagine an object or concept of some kind, and describe it in detail.

Exercise 4

The aim of this exercise is to develop inner consciousness, and the link with the past and the future as part of a general and multidimensional formation.

Some kind of scene or event must be imagined in detail, as well as everything that preceded the event (the reasons, conditions, and so on). The future of the event and its repercussions must also be imagined. Of course, it is preferable to concentrate on positive events.

Exercise 5

An exercise for developing self-reflection.

Some kind of object must be imagined, and its "process" of growth - the beginning of its existence - must be examined via its growth and development. Afterward, the character of the person himself must be visualized; the growth of his private "I" from the beginning of life must be examined in perspective, up to the possibilities that are latent in his personal growth and blooming.

Exercise 6

An exercise for inner conscious awareness.

Imagine the soul as some kind of object, preferably as a flower that opens up to absorb life's good influence.

Exercise 7

Imagine a sensory activity from inside one of the senses (that is, from an "internal" point of view), in other words, concentrate on the senses of smell, taste, sight, touch, and hearing, and try to experience them without using them, with the whole activity being a visualization.

Exercise 8

A meditation exercise that relates to the internal link between man and the elements of the universe that contain life energies: water, fire, air, and earth.

Breathe deep, correct breaths, relax, and bring the body to a high degree of inner awareness by visualizing using the senses of smell, touch, taste, sight, and hearing. Imagine a particular event that includes one of the elements, and activate the inner consciousness in order to experience all the aspects of the event with the five senses (for example, walking barefoot on the shore).

Concluding meditation

Concentrate and return to reality, all the while feeling your personal physical existence.

It must be remembered that good health and physical fitness are beneficial to the overall activity of the body, since the improvement and nurturing of every layer of the body - that is, development of the awareness of a particular layer - support and lead to a sensitivity to the rest of the layers; the person as a whole is an entire unit that combines all the layers.

Because channeling is the development of the sensitive part of our nature, the exercises should help raise the consciousness of the world around us by means of spiritual sensation, and then, ostensibly, we will not need our senses in order to experience things: we can do this from our inner beings in a profound and authentic way.

Some people need reinforcement in order to do meditation, since they are skeptical, or have weak characters. Those people should perform meditation in the company of people with whom they feel comfortable - better still, when they share a common aim.

Below is the procedure for an improved group meditation:

The meditation should be performed in a circle consisting of at least four people, in order to create the required power of energy. One of the group should be an experienced meditation guide (or capable "medium").

The intentions of the meditation should be defined, so as to reach a decision pertaining to the direction of the meditation. Every kind of meditation requires a different plan of action, as well as a different kind of energy during the activity.

A time must be set for performing the meditation, and thereafter the meditation must be repeated every week at the same time. The participants must be there a few minutes before beginning the meditation, since in fact an "appointment" has been made with the spirit, so punctuality is advised. In addition, this interval of time will allow people to relax and create the necessary pause between the frenzied activities of the day and the required concentration during meditation. The conversation between the participants must not relate to the events of the day, but should be a preparation for the forthcoming spiritual activity, and focus on the approaching meditation.

It is recommended that the participants refrain from drinking before meditation - especially caffeine, which is liable to harm concentration.

The order of the meeting should be determined during the first meeting. Every participant has his fixed place, which is reserved for him throughout the series of meetings, except if the guide or medium feels that some kind of movement of energy is required.

During meditation, the content and the explanation of the messages transmitted must not be discussed. This will prevent conversations between group members during meditation.

When the meditation is over, no more messages should be transmitted.

A fixed order must be set for the meditation activity. Every group is entitled to determine the order of its activities, but the order that is fixed should be followed throughout all the meetings. The recommended order is as follows:

Opening words
Addressing the "spirit" (that is, declaring the aim of the meditation)
Joint meditation
Transmitting messages with the "spirit"
Conclusion

The average time for the meditation is 40 minutes. It should not be longer than that, and a balanced return to reality should be observed.

A great deal of patience is required during meditation, as well as a lot of intense work and a high degree of self-discipline. It is important to remember that meditation is joint work with the "spirit," and it is vital to reach completion and compatibility with it.

* * *

After they had spent some time working on chakra-balancing and aura-viewing exercises, Julie, Brandon, Mike, Jarron, Tracy, and Trevor decided to begin meditation exercises. They decided on a fixed day and time, once a week, for their meetings. Each one found his or her own space for meditating, but when they worked in couples, they made sure to switch partners each time, in order to undergo as great a variety of experiences as possible, and encounter the different energies of the members of the group. Brandon's mother, Stella, who was a medium, was asked to lead the group because of her profound knowledge of the exercises and her strong spiritual affinity.

One of the exercises that most excited the group was the one for self-development. In this exercise, each member of the group had to imagine some object from the beginning of its existence, through its gradual development, comparing the development of the object to the development of the personal "I" of each group member. The choice of object could be conscious, but it was preferable that, after doing the first exercise, in which correct, conscious breathing was practiced, the body and muscles were relaxed, and the body and consciousness were prepared for the following exercises, the person *feel* the appropriate object whose development was to be imagined during the exercise for self-development.

During this exercise, in fact, some of the group members already knew what object they would imagine during the meditation. Stella, as an experienced medium, explained to the group that it was possible that the development and growth of this object, which was, in fact, analogous to their own development, would not be smooth and optimistic, and was liable to encounter certain obstacles. It was important to know that those barriers represent the various barriers in a person's development, and it was very important to imagine them disappearing, while the developing object flourished in a beautiful and harmonious way and overcame all the obstacles. The members of the group had many interesting experiences.

During the first meditation exercise, Tracy, who had suddenly and intuitively felt that she was a flower, chose to see a flower as the object that reflected her personal development. After she had relaxed her body, taken slow, deep, calm breaths, and closed her eyes, she felt how she entered little by little into a calm, pleasant meditative state. In her mind's eye, she saw a little seed buried in the earth. The earth was hard and dry, and Tracy felt that it was not easy for the little seed to try and burst out. After it had sprouted a tiny root into the earth, it tried to grow upward, sprouting a frail stalk while it was still in the earth.

She felt as if rock-hard earth was crushing the seed, so she sent warmth and love to it, and encouraged it to continue sprouting. And indeed, little by little, the thin stalk began to push its way upward inside the earth, while the delicate roots continued to descend into the belly of the earth slowly but surely. She watched how the stalk sprouted its first tiny leaf, and she felt as if she really was the plant itself. She experienced the wonder of the tender plant when it felt the pleasant light of the sun, the gentle wind that caressed its stalk, and the warm earth beneath its roots. Slowly the plant sprouted another leaf, and a little bud emerged at the tip of its stalk.

Tracy felt fascinated, as if the plant itself didn't know what would come out of that bud, and was astonished at its very beauty and strength. The plant was delicate and small, but began to feel stronger and more confident as more tiny leaves sprouted. Gradually, the plant's roots lengthened in the earth, and the little green bud began to open amazingly slowly.

Suddenly, Tracy felt that the plant was having a hard time getting the bud to open, because it was thirsty, and there was a kind of dryness in its stalk that was parching it and exhausting it. Although no thought had passed through Tracy's mind during the entire meditation, she knew intuitively that it was another of those obstacles that she had to overcome. In her imagination, it was even as if she was not in control of this imaginary "script," and she saw a kind of manna of golden droplets of light falling and encompassing the plant, enveloping the stalk and the leaves that were absorbing them, and sinking into the earth until they reached the roots, which drank the golden droplets thirstily.

A marvelous feeling of strength and vitality spread through her body. The little bud began to open slowly, revealing the first petals of a flower, which stretched out and became thin, delicate and resilient petals in a stunningly beautiful purple-lilac color. The gentle wind bent the flower's strong, pliant stalk a little, caressing the delicate petals. The flower's whole being felt that the universe was beneficent and loving to everything in it. Droplets of light in various colors fell on it lightly every now and then, and some of them were absorbed by the flower, while some enveloped the flower in their light. It was a wondrous experience.

Brandon also saw himself as a seed, but it was a big, brown seed that burst through the earth's surface quickly and powerfully. The development of the stalk was also fast, and its roots, which penetrated deeply into the earth, were strong and thick. The strong, green plant soon took the form of a tree, whose trunk gradually broadened, and grew thick branches.

However, to Brandon's surprise, even after the tree was big and strong, it had no leaves whatsoever. In his imagination, Brandon saw how the tree sprouted leaves, and he encouraged it, enveloping it in a pleasant, green aura, until the first leaves began to appear. It was a long process, and even after the tree was laden with green leaves, Brandon had to encourage it to bear fruit. It seemed that, just like in Brandon's own life, bearing fruit was not easy to do. But Brandon did not give up. It seemed that he only had to make a small effort for the tree to continue by itself, bearing many types of fruit that Brandon had never seen in his life. At a certain point, a sudden growth spurt occurred, and the tree was filled with a variety of fruit and colorful flowers simultaneously. Songbirds fluttered around it, and landed on its branches, enjoying its sweet fruits, and giving the tree a tremendous feeling of happiness and fulfillment.

The other members of the group also experienced wonderful things. Jarron saw himself as a baby bird. He had no idea what this nestling would develop into, as it had to contend with considerable difficulties while it was growing up, but ultimately it became a large, amazingly beautiful, multicolored songbird, with a long, golden tail that opened up like a fan in a myriad of colors. At first, the bird had a hard time making itself heard, but when its voice finally emerged, it was incredibly beautiful and delicate. Jarron noted that the only bird he knew of that in any way resembled the bird he had seen during his meditation, was the exquisite and colorful bird of paradise.

The rest of the group members also had interesting and stimulating experiences during the meditation. For some, their process of development was easier and smoother. Others were forced to overcome difficult obstacles and setbacks at various stages. When they looked inside themselves, they could find the same obstacles in their own lives. Some of the obstacles belonged to the past, and as for those that had not yet been overcome - now the members of the group had the tools to deal with them, along with increasing their spiritual awareness.

After the meditation session, the members of the group performed various grounding exercises, such as standing firmly on the ground, jumping, and swinging their arms. Stella summed up the session in a few words. She did not, however, mention the beneficent beings that had been present at the session and had helped the group cope with the obstacles. She had seen some of them, but she knew that there was a time and a place for everything.

Performing Channeling

Stage 1:
Preparations for performing channeling

The meaning of channeling is man's identifying with spirituality by means of color, symbols, or any other unique phenomenon. Channeling is also powerful energy that awakens in the person.

By means of the symbol or the color that suits the person, he becomes aware of the light, to identifying his inner being, to linking up with his subconscious.

All the symbols, colors, messages, or sensations that emerge at the same time in the channeler can be seen or felt, and they constitute the action of channeling.

If the linking does not occur during the first attempt, it is possible to repeat the action several times (like "redial" on the phone), since every additional attempt to raise the experience to the conscious level increases the depth and enrichment of the awareness until it reaches consciousness.

Channeling is performed only after preparatory exercises (during which unplanned channeling could occur).

In addition, it must be pointed out once again that channeling must be done in a controlled way, in stages, and by constructing the correct foundations and understanding of the processes that are performed.

First stages of channeling

In order to channel, you must define the intention of the channeling, that is, determine objectives. The objectives must be positive and unselfish, because if negative energies are activated as a result of the channeling, they will have a boomerang effect on the channeler.

Correct nutrition will assist in balancing the body in order to create the required harmony in the body. You should not drink too much, or eat too much meat; it is preferable to eat chicken or fish - this will facilitate metabolism. You should not use much sugar or salt, and avoid fats. However, try to consume a lot of olive oil, fruits and vegetables. Natural grains are also recommended. Learn to eat slowly and calmly. Correct and nourishing eating will enhance the body's health and the attainment of self-control, and will improve the balance between the physical energy of the body and the spiritual energy inside it.

Refrain from smoking and drinking alcohol for 12 hours before beginning channeling, as well as from taking drugs; this will preserve self-control and stability during channeling.

Refrain from sexual relations before channeling, in order to preserve your physical strength and balance. In addition, it must be pointed out that you may experience sexual excitement during channeling. This excitement can be controlled by means of spreading the sexual energy throughout the chakras.

The body should be strengthened with vitamins.

Objects with a magnetic or electric field should be removed from the body in order to prevent an "electric shock" as a result of energies that emanate from the body during channeling.

You must be very patient, since spiritual and mental

obstacles are liable to delay the success of the channeling temporarily.

You must be well grounded, and center yourself well at the beginning of the channeling process. Do not lose your self-control for a second.

When you finish channeling, see that you stabilize yourself and get your feet back onto solid ground - literally.

Stick to a fixed daily routine in order to preserve your body's balance and stability, and to keep the influences of negative energies at bay.

Stage 2:
Preparations before channeling

Before beginning the preparations for channeling, it is important to point out that you must overcome the doubts in your heart. These doubts are legitimate, and are even desirable at the beginning stage of the decision to perform channeling. Every change in a person's life arouses skepticism, anxiety, and insecurity, and you must overcome and restrain that aspect that rejects channeling, but not subdue it, because sometimes it is vital for toning down the enthusiasm that is liable to cause damage. In its capacity as "watchdog," skepticism will control the rate of the channeling.

Your personality must adapt itself to the change that is expected after channeling, and speeding up the activity or over-enthusiasm is liable to upset your stability.

An excess of energies is liable to undermine your mental and physical stability. Exaggerated channeling is also likely to cause damage, especially to the nervous system, and from the point of view of mental exhaustion.

The process should be started by drinking liquids, in order to prevent dryness that may occur as a result of the experience that is about to happen, and in order to stimulate the rate of the energies in the body. As we mentioned before, you should refrain from eating so as not to make the body heavy and tired. It is recommended that the channeling be performed in a comfortable and intimate room in which you (and your partner) will not be disturbed. Soft lighting, quiet music, and a fragrant essential oil are likely to contribute to a moving experience. It is important to see that pets are removed from the area, since they have strong energies, and are liable to disrupt the smooth course of the experience.

Sit comfortably in the middle of the room. The positions recommended for meditation are completely suitable for performing channeling. Regulate your breathing, relax, and feel comfortable and secure.

Center yourself by visualizing your feet placed firmly on one of the previously mentioned symbols for activating a high degree of concentration - the one that you prefer - and continue broadening your consciousness of the symbol throughout the entire volume of the room. While doing so, focus on the negative energies, and also determine a time limit for the experience.

You should link up with your partner by means of concentrating on a particular object or concept, which has been defined as a focal point for both partners, and visualize a bubble that envelops both of you.

Relax. Breathe deeply and steadily and concentrate until you feel an awareness of every part of your body, beginning with the soles of your feet and your legs, and then on to every single part of your body.

Stage 3:
Developing awareness

As we mentioned previously, learning channeling is done with a partner, who serves as a protector for the channeler.

At this point, the partner - the protector - must remain aware in order to safeguard you - the channeler. The protection is spiritual, and you can be helped by white, blue, or gold, or any other symbol. You must concentrate, be conscious of the magnetic atmosphere surrounding you, rise to a higher level of awareness, that is, penetrate the subconscious of your being, but not break the contact with your partner - the protector. Although you have penetrated into another sphere, you must not detach yourself from reality; in other words, you should talk to your partner and keep in contact with him in order to preserve the terrestrial link.

At this stage, you must open yourself up to what is happening around you, but not start analyzing things logically, or assess the situation; rather, absorb the experience as it is.

The channeling experience will be individual. You can see colors, smell odors, hear sounds, experience abstract symbols or concepts, and even experience a presence in the area that could well be your inner being, or a foreign element.

* * *

We can see an example of the use of symbols for protection in the work of Sally and Joanna. Before starting the channeling, Sally wanted to protect herself with a Star of David. She sat facing the east, relaxed her body, took deep, calm breaths, closed her eyes, emptied her mind of all thoughts, and entered a state of meditation. Joanna stood behind her, with her eyes open, imagining a huge golden Star of David in a horizontal position, completely surrounding Sally. Sally was in the middle of it. This system of protection is extremely effective, as it links the "higher beings" and the "lower beings." (The inverted triangle symbolizes the terrestrial, the human, man, while the regular triangle symbolizes the upper, spiritual worlds. The combination of the two triangles represents the desire for a link between man and the Divine.)

Joanna decided to use color to protect herself before channeling. Gold is an extremely strong color, and for this reason, Joanna chose to use it. She filled herself with it - which was in fact tantamount to filling herself with pure spiritual energies. After relaxing her body, she sat calmly facing the east (many practitioners of channeling prefer this direction, because of its positive energies), took a few deep breaths, and gently moved her arms over her head and body, in order to sense the vibrations of her aura. After this preparation, she began to imagine her aura while she was enveloped in and surrounded by a large ellipse of golden light. She inhaled some of the golden ellipse, drawing the golden light inside her, and exhaled it again, filling and protecting herself with light. This method is also effective and safe to use before channeling, and not only protects the person from undesirable energies, but also fills him or her with pure divine energies.

Vic preferred to use prayer as a protection while channeling. He would relax and enter a state of meditation. Then, since he linked up with spiritual beings containing Jewish energies during his channeling, he would stand calmly and steadily, and address a sincere request to God to cleanse him of any superfluous thought or emotion, and to fill him with the energy of love. Above his head, he saw the letters that comprise the holy name, in a combination of white and gold. From the holy name, he saw a pleasant stream of shining white light that flowed into his body via his spinal column from above, and left his body through the soles of his feet into the depths of the earth, for grounding. From the depths of the earth, the white light emerged and enveloped him in a protective bubble. After this preparation, Vic felt ready to begin channeling.

Channeling

Stage 1

Use a quiet, pleasant room. Choose a sitting position that is comfortable for you (see previous descriptions in exercises), relax, and, in order to make the experience more profound, close your eyes.

Breathe deeply, and regulate the rate of your breathing. Concentrate and imagine how your inner consciousness descends and penetrates the earth (all the while breathing deeply and steadily). At this stage, the conscious awareness is resting (is planted) somewhere inside the earth, bound to the elements of nature. This consciousness begins to grow in brilliant shades and an abundance of light, and becomes concentrated in one ray that ascends from inside the earth to the sole of your right foot. Now you must focus on this area of the foot, feel the power of the experience, and lead the ray up along the length of your body via your right palm. Hold the ray on your right shoulder while focusing on the feelings that emanate from the whole right side of your body, and the feeling of the light that is radiated from that area. Transfer the ray of light to the left shoulder and experience the awareness of that side. Direct the ray downward, via your left palm, your fingers, to your left foot, and, feeling the power of the experience, lower the ray from the sole of your left foot into the earth, and let it link up with the starting point. After the circle is closed, the light continues its movement and ascends the right side of your body (while you are taking deep, regular breaths), and descends the left side in order to complete an additional circle.

It is possible to experience the energies that surround your body, and the bestowing of vitality and energy on your inner being, by means of deep, steady breathing. You should allow the energy to make at least seven "circles."

Stage 2

Concentrate, and experience another ray - preferably in a different color - that emerges from the earth to the center of the body in the direction of the column or line of the seven chakras. This ray is saturated with whirling energy, and its spinning causes the negative energies, such as fears or other negative barriers, to disintegrate and disappear. The chakras open gradually, and the ray passes through them in an upward direction toward the crown, and from there outward, when the whole body is illuminated, and the ray surrounds it entirely and protects it from negative energies that are liable to "fall" back after they have been ejected from the crown.

Stage 3

Visualize a ray ascending in the direction of the crown, when this time the crown chakra draws/sucks the ray upward. Now you must find a comfortable place where the awareness can "rest." Visualize a passage that leads to a door, for which only you, the channeler, hold the key. In this room, which is a kind of "holy of holies" for you, there are "objects" that are of interest only to you, and you feel comfortable with them. These can be scenes from nature, a particular figure, feelings, memories, and so on.

In the middle of the room there is a pool containing a reservoir of shining light. You must go into the light, dip yourself and disappear in it, and then imagine that a figure of white, shining light comes out and ascends from inside the water. This is the embodiment and manifestation of the "inner I," the exposure of awareness, which is saturated with perfect, unconditional love. You must welcome this figure, and accompany it. Since you are apparently detached from the thought factor, you can experience the inner awareness of your existence without the limitations of judgment or factual analysis. At this stage, it is possible to feel the merging with the "inner I," and the joining of the flowing energies.

Stage 4

You, the channeler, who are experiencing and are aware of your existence, imagine the return of the figure of light to the pool, your body leaving the water, going out of the room, and, following the ray that brought you here, returning to the physical existence of your body, via the crown chakra.

At this stage, you should breathe deeply, and examine the nature of the feelings that emerge. After calming down for a few minutes, open your eyes, and write down the whole sequence of the process and the attendant emotional experiences.

Those who are focusing on channeling should close their eyes when they have finished writing, and, accompanied by the "inner I," should return to the room and direct the "inner I" into the pool of light from which it emerged during the process, and experience the sensation that this awareness is easily accessible, and can help in times of need.

You can linger for some time in the room, and you can go out and return a second time. After all, this is the place where you, the channeler, experience true freedom and release from every limitation. And again, by means of the ray, you must return to your body via the crown chakra, and return the awareness to inside your physical body.

This technique of channeling by means of the personification of properties greatly facilitates the experience, but it also ensures that the conscious awareness does not abandon the body during channeling, and permits the process to be halted at any moment. There is always the fear that people are liable to lose their self-control, and be carried away and harmed, and for that reason, channeling must not be done without prior preparations, or without releasing negative energies.

During the process, the power of the channeling depends on the channeler himself. If the level of the experience is insufficient, it can be raised by greater devotion, and if the power is too strong, it can be restrained or the power of its energy decreased. Alternatively, the experience can be terminated entirely. The experience occurs at a high level of awareness, with a sensation of the creation of a bond, which is manifested in an individual way, according to the nature of the channeler. Sometimes it is a question of picking up an alien presence, or sounds and colors; in general, there is a sensation of a need to express some kind of message. If some kind of figure appears, it is possible to ask it questions about where it comes from, its nature, and any other question that the channeler is curious about, in order to deepen the connection between the channeler and the spiritual experience.

In fact, *binding energy* is created here between the channeler and the experience (the unconscious layer of his experience), and as a result of the connection, the channeler's understanding and awareness increase, and bring the unconscious closer to the conscious.

To channel means having a higher level of awareness after channeling than before channeling - that is, to improve awareness.

Channeling requires learning, constant practice, and understanding of the process. Channeling is expressed in every one of the aspects of life. Every action that is performed with suitable inspiration, and with concentration, will bring "improvement" in its wake. After some time, there is no need to invest conscious thought energy in achieving the experience; it becomes an unconscious centering. The only thing necessary for it is to be in full self-control, not to allow oneself to be carried away, and not to feel that the ground is disappearing from under one's feet.

The more one's awareness increases, the shadows, that is, the negative energies, diminish; the person is more aware of his existence, and can balance his life more easily.

Concluding Channeling

In general, channeling should be concluded after about twenty minutes, and the channeler should return to reality. This must be done with the carefully controlled release of the spiritual energies, focusing once more on the body's physical energies, releasing oneself from the energies of the aura, and concentrating on the physical awareness of each and every part of the body. The channeler must increase his awareness of the physical energies, and stabilize them, balance the body, and return to everyday reality.

No hard and fast rules should be made for practicing the channeling experience, since the experience is individual, but it is a good idea to do the exercises at fixed times. In general, a week of practice is sufficient for undergoing the experience, but some people need a longer time than that.

* * *

Andy, a holistic healer who was involved with the more physical aspects of holistic healing, decided to expand his consciousness, and a few years after the world of the spirit and energies had opened up before him, he decided to try channeling. After he had faithfully practiced the preparatory exercises for channeling for a few weeks, he began to work on balancing his chakras. This process was a bit tiresome for him: as a consequence of his genuine concentration on himself, and the process of balancing, many unpleasant experiences from his childhood flooded into his mind. By means of the ability to see things in proportion and from a distance, which he acquired from the preparatory exercises and the developing spiritual consciousness that accompanied them, he succeeded in dealing with those traumatic experiences. Now he understood why they had occurred, and he taught himself, in a clear and conscious way, to forgive the people who had hurt him.

This process took some time, but Andy felt its action and results in every facet of life. He began to understand many problems whose essence he had previously been unable to explain, such as his inability to maintain an intimate relationship with one partner, his frequent job changes, and his obvious tendency to run away and constantly be on the move. He succeeded in understanding how and from where he had acquired these characteristics.

In addition, he worked on his irascibility; he was quick-tempered, and would react with irritability and sharpness to every little thing. He learned to understand that his ego, which seemed to be strong and confident, actually felt weak and small, and anger was one of its easy ways of defending itself.

The exercises for balancing the chakras proved to be extremely effective. More and more, Andy learned how to understand his inner self, while remaining faithful to his desire for good, and he knew that he was responsible for choosing how to react to events. If they had occurred in the past, he taught himself to forgive and understand them; if they were occurring in the present, he was learning to see them in the correct proportion, from a point of view of calmness and serenity, to look for the good in every person, to understand, and to humble himself.

In order to learn how to feel his own and other people's auras as an extra benefit in self-development, and as an additional tool in the treatments he administered, he joined a healing group that concentrated on seeing and feeling the aura. Gradually, he learned to feel and sense auras very easily. His visual ability also increased and strengthened, and at a certain stage, he could see auras, but not in color - rather, just as an energy field of a certain width. Using colors, symbols or prayer as protection, he practiced every day, and felt how the methods of protection enabled him to filter all the energies that reached him, and to absorb only the good and the positive ones.

Andy did not neglect the physical aspects, either. He gradually stopped smoking, and learned how to eat nutritiously, both of which affected his life positively. Along the way, he also lost the considerable excess weight he had been carrying for years, and his physical abilities improved when he learned to love and accept his body. He made sure that he participated in light athletic activities and power walking on a daily basis.

When he felt that he was ready to begin channeling, Andy was at a far higher spiritual and physical level than he had been before he had set out on his conscious spiritual saga.

The changes that had occurred in him were evident in all facets of his life, ultimately causing him to be a person who was more aware and serene, as well as full of love and compassion.

When he set out to begin channeling, he defined his intention clearly. Andy felt that the aim of channeling for him was the acceptance of divine, spiritual enlightenment and spiritual knowledge. This would further his spiritual growth, concomitantly developing his ability to heal his patients more fully, and would help him to transmit this enlightenment and information to his patients and his friends, too. It would assist their personal growth, and in that way, of course, help to bring the world into a more balanced state, aspiring to good and truth. Andy's intentions should not be taken lightly. Since they were extremely sincere, the universe reacted to the frequencies of love and sharing that Andy transmitted, and he did indeed receive a great deal of help from the universe, in every facet of his life and spiritual development.

Since he knew that he was liable to drift off easily, and was not overly connected to the earth, he asked his friend Alex to help him perform channeling by sitting with him in the room and doing the protection exercises together with him. Little did he know that his choice and request were astonishingly accurate, because, as Andy found out later, he certainly did receive marvelous enlightenment, which he succeeded in vocalizing to Alex, but after the channeling, he had difficult expressing it in an orderly fashion. Fortunately for him, Alex was an excellent listener, and remembered every word that Andy uttered.

For about five hours before the channeling, Andy made sure not to eat anything, as five hours previously he had eaten a full, balanced meal. He chose a room in his house with a pleasant atmosphere, and there he spent a long time in meditation. (A place in which meditation is performed on a regular basis retains the meditative atmosphere, and if it is kept clean and pure, the person finds it much easier to enter into a state of meditation and channeling quickly.)

In the room, Andy prepared an essential oil burner, using frankincense, which is known for its abilities to help people open up spiritually (this oil was even used in the Temple, and it is used to this day in temples all over the world). Andy placed a large, purified quartz crystal on one of the shelves, and it transmitted and disseminated positive vibrations throughout the entire room.

The energy of friendship and affection that existed between Andy and Alex was also felt in the room. Energy of this type constitutes protection in itself against non-positive forces, and helps draw light and love to the people in the room.

Andy sat down on the floor, and placed a cushion beneath him to make himself more comfortable. Both he and Alex relaxed their bodies and muscles, and took deep, conscious, but calm breaths. They agreed that the protection they would invoke would be a big blue, white and gold Star of David, which Alex would "transmit" to Andy, while Andy imagined it in his mind's eye. Both of them saw Andy sitting in the middle of the big Star of David beneath him, sending rays of blue, gold and white light from its six points all over the room. Andy felt strong but pleasant vibrations encompassing him and enveloping him in a protective bubble of golden-white light. He began to transmit his inner consciousness deep into the earth, while creating a harmonious link with the many elements that he felt. He saw flashes of pictures of the inner depths of the earth in his head; he saw the eddyings of its heart, the metamorphosis of stones, and various events that were occurring in its bowels.

Alex, who saw that Andy was focusing on these visions for a long time, and knew that this was not his ultimate aim, sent him some light energy to arouse and center him, and this encouraged Andy to continue the meditation. Now he felt a colored ray of light, which was a combination of many lights, rising from within the earth to his right foot, flowing along the right side of his body, in a warm, pleasant current. Little by little, the ray flowed to the left side of his body, and he moved it down across his right foot, feeling the light flowing through all his organs. His hands became very warm, and the rate of his breathing accelerated slightly. Consciously, he calmed and regulated his breathing, and imagined how the ray of light was descending into the earth in an outline of a perfect circle around his body. With each breath, he felt how he was filled with light, and with each exhalation, he felt as if he was expelling everything that he didn't need, or that was liable to disturb him. He continued taking deep, slow, regular breaths, and enjoyed the feeling of his body being filled with energy.

Now Andy began to imagine a ray of purple light rising from the earth and flowing inside his spinal column in fast spiraling motions. He felt as if many blockages were being released as the ray made its way up his spine, using its warmth and lightness to eliminate every blockage and obstacle in its path. Wherever the ray passed on its way upward, it radiated light into Andy's organs. When the purple light flowed into his head, Andy felt how it enveloped his brain, creating a perfect balance between the right and left hemispheres.

He concentrated on the picture of the light flowing through his head, and saw it fill little holes and get rid of little black spots in various regions of his brain. Although he did not know the significance of this technique, this state of channeling caused him to reach the balance of the two hemispheres of his brain, at the same time eliminating blockages and filling hollows. He felt his whole body surrounded and illuminated by delicate purple light, which reverberated gently, soothing and filling him. He concentrated on what was happening in his head, and on the crown chakra, which was now open and sensitive to picking up and receiving messages.

At this point, while his eyes were still closed, he imagined a long, white corridor, filled with a kind of shining white light. He felt himself moving along it, until he reached a big golden door. He touched it, and it opened at his touch. Opposite him lay a scene of breathtaking beauty. There was a gigantic green expanse in which there were a number of ancient trees, spreading their branches over a blue lake, which glittered in the warm rays of the sun.

He saw a straight-backed, white-haired, and handsome old man approaching him with slow steps. Wordlessly, the old man led him to the lake, which lay before him in all its glory. Andy saw himself entering the transparent blue waters of the lake, felt the waters flowing around him, pleasant and warm. These waters were the waters of consciousness. He felt them flowing over his head, enveloping him, and embracing his whole being. As he was about to get out of the lake, a shining white figure, pure and floating, emerged. Andy joined the figure, which led him to a shady corner and instructed him to leave his brain - the analytical and critical intelligence that interfered with the reception of the delicate, intuitive messages that have to be absorbed without thought - in a wooden box decorated with golden fittings. The box opened by itself, and after Andy had placed his brain in it, it closed automatically. For a moment, a wave of anxiety overcame him. But the figure caused a feeling of peace to flow into him, and he actually felt as if it was flowing from him and was inside him.

At the same time, Alex, who was following the movements of Andy's closed eyes, transmitted love and confidence to help him along the rest of his way. Andy felt whole and perfect. Now he was ready to sit opposite the old man, whose face was radiating warmth and light, and seemed very familiar to him. Little by little, the old man began to tell Andy various stories. As if in a dream, Andy, mumbling, repeated the words he heard, although the old man was speaking silently. Alex, who was listening attentively to what Andy was saying, noticed that his voice was slightly different, deeper, slow, calm, and very relaxed. The old man revealed messages to Andy concerning his vocation in the world and the things he must fix in this incarnation.

After a time, which seemed very long to Andy, but, as Alex said afterward, was no longer than nine or ten minutes, Andy saw the old man rise and begin to lead him back to the old tree, at the foot of which lay the wooden box. The moment Andy stood next to it, he understood that he had to "reinstate" his regular rational consciousness. The box opened by itself, and Andy felt that he was slowly coming back to himself. He saw himself bidding the old man farewell. The old man blessed him lovingly, and slowly joined the shining white ray of light once more. It passed through the crown of his head, slowly descended the entire length of his body, stimulating all the organs it passed through, until it went through Andy's feet and returned to the depths of the earth.

Andy remained seated, eyes closed, for a few minutes, and little by little began to open his eyes. He smiled at Alex, and felt wide awake, calm and serene. After resting briefly, he sat with Alex and discussed his experience with him, reminding himself of the important aspects of enlightenment that had come his way, and working out how he could apply them in daily life.

* * *

Karen, who had been involved in channeling for a number of years, said that in most of her experiences, she saw a dim purple light, through which she could distinguish non-human figures that were practicing various techniques in the use of crystals.

Following her first attempts at channeling, she understood that she had to broaden her knowledge about the use of crystals. She began to work with them, and quickly understood that the visions that she saw during channeling were describing exceptional techniques - very ancient or very modern, she could not tell - in the use of crystals.

She succeeded in applying some of the healing techniques she saw in her visions to more up-to-date methods of using crystals, and in using them for healing purposes. Gradually, as she got more deeply involved in channeling, she advanced and became a practitioner who used crystals and healing stones, which she combined with healing and Reiki.

She had amazing experiences of "help during treatment." It happened that while she was treating one of her patients, she saw in her mind's eye the room surrounded by hundreds of strange and rare crystals, unusual stones which were placed on her patient's body, rays of light in different colors that flowed to her patient via her consciousness, as well as other methods of healing that were unfamiliar to her, and helped her when she was administering treatment. The interesting thing was that many patients in fact "felt" the things she saw in her visions. For instance, when she saw a giant ruby lying on the base chakra of a patient, he told her afterward that he had felt a large, healing object, which radiated warmth and light, lying on his base chakra! These visions, the fruits of channeling, were very useful to her in her treatments, and made them more effective.

The Influences of Channeling

The positive influences

The first level of channeling is the connection that is created as a result of the passage of energies between the various layers of the body (a combination of physical and spiritual energies), and at the second level, it is the connection that is created with cosmic energies.

This channeling brings in its wake a change in the channeler's personality and a different view of the nature of man in the cosmic whole.

Channeling brings in its wake a broadening of awareness and understanding, mental peace, and *joie de vivre*, a correct view of life in general, and a merging of man in the "current of life."

The linking of the unconscious and the conscious leads to a clearer and more natural awareness, which enables the channeler to make decisions more easily and correctly, increases his creativity, and facilitates its expression (since the linking exposes properties such as artistic talent, intellectual depth, and so on, that were trapped in the channeler's soul, and had not been manifested previously). Channeling renews the channeler's energies, and provides him with the truth he needs, while affording a more profound understanding of other people.

Every person has a soul, and a beating heart, which forgives, understands, and loves. Channeling liberates the channeler from the bonds of selfishness and personal interests, raises the awareness of personal ability and the consciousness that it is possible to live a life filled with content and realization.

In addition (although the right to absolute forgiveness resides in the hands of a superior power, God), channeling brings about the understanding and recognition that the right to forgive, love, and so on, is located within us, as is fear, which causes the person to feel threatened. In fact, fear is an important tool in this system, because the recognition that fear is part of our existence allows a door to improvement to be opened. Channeling opens those doors, dismantles obstacles, and permits a clear and true view of the elements that dictate our lives, that is, a clear and correct view of the fear within us.

Channeling affords release from and use of the elements that inhibit our lives.

Many of us are bound to past memories, even though we tend to flee from memories of failure, and deny them in an attempt to prevent physical and mental pain. However, these events can serve us by means of their very release, when the aim is to live a full life in the present, without residual elements, and without limitations that block future development.

The release of a blockage of a different kind is how we relate to life and death. His whole life, man fears and dreads the moment of his death, and represses thoughts about death. (However, they pop up over and over again and disturb his life.) Channeling, which broadens man's understanding, enables him to understand that his death means the death of his body, in order to be reborn as a new soul. Death is an event that occurs *in* life, and not *to* life; it is a part of life.

Channeling establishes the link between the individual and society - especially in the present era, in which the emphasis is placed on the development of the individual. Channeling exposes the inner being of the individual to the collective consciousness, leading to universal understanding by means of diverting the attention from the "individual I" to "we."

In the wake of channeling, the difficult struggles with life's vicissitudes - such as the loss of loved ones, overcoming physical pain, release from tension, and so on - become easier.

The more the awareness resulting from channeling broadens, the more the recognition of being and the general truth spreads. This is a natural part of the growth of the channeler's consciousness. There is no need, nor is it possible, to see the general truth at first glance. The truth that is accessible to the eyes of the channeler is *his* absolute truth, but it will broaden as long as his consciousness goes deeper and his development broadens. That is, the more he penetrates into the unconscious corners within him, his understanding - or his truth - will grow.

One of the results of channeling is attaining freedom. Freedom is not a physical state. Freedom is consciousness that liberates man from fears, from religious and cultural conventions, and so on. Freedom liberates man from the bonds of strict morality, and permits freedom of choice of a way of life. Internal awareness is what leads to understanding, and prevents fear of the unknown. Identification with our inner being presents the correct choice in life, and prevents the fears of the residual elements that lead to the wrong choice. Freedom, which leads to the correct choice, takes man beyond his private ego, and beyond the pressures that are liable to limit his freedom - to the path of true liberation.

Channeling leads to *joie de vivre. Joie de vivre* is defined as an inner property (that is created as a result of external circumstances). In fact, it is one of the most significant properties in a person's life. Without *joie de vivre*, he has no purpose, and his life continues gloomily and meaninglessly. Even when there is a purpose and a direction in life, it generally does not come to fruition. Channeling affords the understanding of the significance of man's *joie de vivre*, and brings it to a significant level in his life.

Channeling occurs as a result of the passage of energies between the various layers in the body, that is, the merging of the physical and spiritual energies.

Every part of the body participates in the flow of energies, and the channeler is aware of each and every detail of his organs - both physical and mental. The energies accelerate the body's rate of activity in order to create the harmony that comes from nature itself, and the awareness of it.

Striving for harmony is what will improve the channeler's life; it will reveal life's positive sides; in addition, it will supply the requisite tools for coping with problems, and not bypassing and ignoring them.

While striving for higher spheres is the aim of many channelers, in general, people perform channeling because they desire a full, serene life in which they can realize their individual ambitions. The person wants to improve his performance in various aspects of life, and strengthen his weak character traits; in other words, increase his self-confidence and improve his quality of life.

This situation will bring about a change in the channeler's personality, as well as a different view of the nature of man in the cosmic whole.

Channeling liberates man from the doubts that accompany him in his life, and create in him a lack of self-confidence. Skepticism is a factor that inhibits development in life, and prevents the realization of ambitions. But it must be remembered that skepticism is a vital part in the understanding of the channeling process, since its very existence in man's consciousness dictates examinations and questions before knowing and accepting channeling and its results. Only after the "examinations" have been performed, and all the necessary precautions deriving from doubt have been taken, will the bothersome cloud disappear and dissipate, and the light be exposed. The dividing wall between the lack of enlightenment and seeing the truth will be revealed. Channeling can also be explained as the removal of the blockages in the channeler's unconscious. These blockages are mainly negative energies that operate in our personalities, and they are liable to have negative results. Thus their removal releases negative obstacles such as hatred, fear, jealousy, and so on. Moreover, channeling leads to recognizing the difference between people (without comparison and without a negative attitude), and to accepting every person for what he is.

Negative influences

Channeling is liable to cause instability, headaches, a lack of concentration, and a loss of self-confidence, as well as feelings of superiority, problems in interpersonal relations, loneliness, and delusions. This occurs when it is performed without prior preparations and without a controlled return to reality, or when the person suffered from physical or mental disorders even before channeling, and their influence is liable to increase as a result of channeling.

It is therefore important to operate in a controlled and responsible manner during the preparations for channeling, and when returning to everyday reality at its conclusion, as well as to determine clear limits before starting.

* * *

Chris, a young business executive, had become interested in channeling in his youth. As a result of his exaggerated self-confidence, he read about different channeling techniques and decided to "dive in at the deep end" without prior preparation, without balancing his chakras or doing meditation exercises, and without balancing his life in the more physical areas. He was convinced that he could enjoy the channeling experience, but was not wise enough to understand it in depth. He ignored the dangers inherent in it for a person who was not sufficiently balanced or talented, and who had not prepared himself for it properly.

Chris's everyday life was fraught with lack of balance and self-awareness. He was a person who was easily angered, quite selfish, and tended to blame the people around him for everything that happened to him, without taking a look inside himself and checking how he himself had gotten into those situations. Moreover, he was patronizing, behaved contemptuously to people who were "subordinate" to him in status, was intolerant toward minorities or people who were different than him, and lacked understanding of the ways of the universe.

He was not aware that channeling is a means of linking up to the energy of the universe in order to inspire and propagate love, tolerance, and world peace, and that people who do not advocate peace and brotherhood are liable to be harmed by it. He assumed that channeling would augment his powers of telepathy (which does indeed happen after channeling is practiced for a long time), and hoped that it would increase his chances of augmenting his wealth, power, and prestige, not to mention benefit his business.

Spurred on by his self-confidence, he approached the experience of channeling without making any prior preparations, or ensuring that he had a friend or teacher to sit beside him during the procedure. Although he followed the principles of channeling itself meticulously, Chris was apparently not supposed to achieve any success through channeling. However, the forces of the universe have their own ways to show a person the error of his ways.

Because of his impatience, he did not protect himself with symbols, color, or anything else. He performed the channeling in the study of his house after eating a heavy meal, including meat and wine, just a few hours beforehand. He took a few deep breaths, concentrated, and imagined how his inner consciousness was descending down into the depths of the earth and penetrating them, then rose in the form of a ray of light through his right leg, and from there, to the rest of his body. The ray of light that he saw was very unclear, and slightly opaque.

After completing two cycles of light, he felt very weak, tired, and listless. In fact, it was not that he was lacking energy, but the energy that entered him was not clean, and his body was too weak to combat it. But he did not stop. He continued with the channeling, even though he felt unpleasant tremors in his body. At a certain point, when he imagined himself entering a room, he sank into a heavy sleep. This was his subconscious warning him that he was not capable of undergoing the channeling experience consciously, and as a defense, caused him to fall into a deep sleep. His sleep was troubled by bad dreams that were amazingly realistic. He saw terrible, traumatic childhood experiences - long repressed in his subconscious - rising to the surface in the form of dreams. He saw frightening and repelling images, and, at a certain point, awoke in fright, terror-stricken.

Shocked by the awful experience, he took a shower, and went out to a pub with his friends. But the same night, and for several nights after that, he was plagued by terrifying dreams and nightmares, to the point that he was afraid to go to sleep, and even when fatigue overcame him, he still suffered from insomnia as a result of fear. His everyday life also deteriorated; he felt depressed, anxious and lacking in self-confidence during the day, and found it difficult to do his work and relate to people properly.

Finally, after he had confided his distress to one of his friends, he was referred to a professional healer and channeler, who explained to him why exactly he was having those terrible dreams, and noted that every cloud had a silver lining. In Chris's case, he now had no choice but to begin to change the patterns of his consciousness from within, and to perform some profound soul-searching, while working on those same traumas that rose inexorably to the surface, as well as on the way in which he thought and behaved.

Eventually, this difficult experience turned out to be very effective, since Chris succeeded in getting down to some serious self-discovery work, and in changing his thought and behavior patterns. It was just a shame that he had to go through such a torturous procedure as a result of approaching channeling without the appropriate preparation and from the wrong internal starting-point.

* * *

Linda's channeling experiences were quite different from those of Chris. Linda was a woman of about 50, a senior book-keeper in a large company, and the mother of three grown children. She related to channeling very seriously, even though her knowledge of it was limited to what she had heard over coffee with her friends. She knew how to appreciate the truth and potential that lay in channeling, as well as the need to prepare the soul, the body and the spirit in a suitable manner prior to beginning the work.

She spent a long time concentrating on the exercises for meditation and for balancing the chakras. As a result, she noticed extreme changes in every aspect of her life. Before starting these exercises, she was convinced that her view of the world, and everything it involved, was absolutely correct. She did not have sufficient awareness to understand that many of the things she did stemmed in fact from acquired thought and behavior patterns, and not only were they not correct, but they annoyed her and those around her. This was true of her "cleanliness mania," as well as of her tremendous anxiety concerning her children, whom she had overprotected, constantly worrying about them, interfering in every facet of their lives, and forcing them to report their whereabouts to her at any hour of the day or night. Linda was convinced that her role as a mother was to "protect" her children, even at the expense of their becoming independent or amassing personal experience. This situation caused many serious conflicts and rows, at the end of which Linda found herself drained of strength, exhausted, and deeply offended.

The exercises for balancing the chakras began to highlight the very fears that plagued her concerning her children, the true reasons for her cleanliness mania, and the prevalent imbalance in her life. Although she ran her domestic life autocratically, at work she was as timid as a kitten, afraid of voicing her opinion, and prepared to swallow the insult of a relatively low salary, as well as unpleasant working conditions.

After practicing the exercises for meditation and for balancing the chakras for some time, she discovered a boldness in herself that she had not known she possessed, and she suddenly began to stand up for herself assertively. Her fear of not being worthy enough and of never finding another job - the same fear that caused her to suffer the exploitative working conditions in silence - gave way to confidence in her abilities, to the point that she no longer feared explaining to her superiors, from the standpoint of a total belief in her abilities and justifiably high self-esteem, how important and indispensable she was to them, and informing them that if they did not relate to her more seriously and respectfully, they would find themselves minus their senior book-keeper.

While working on balancing her chakras, she understood how the lack of balance had influenced the course of her life. The assertiveness that she had acquired focused on her tolerance and persistence in balancing each chakra, and quickly led to a situation in which she demanded a substantial raise in her salary, as well as her own office. As a result of her new-found determination and confidence, she actually obtained everything she wanted.

Her relationship with the members of her family also changed out of all recognition. She began to relate more tolerantly to her children's different opinions and views of the world, and stopped stuffing achievement-orientation down their throats in the areas in which she thought it was important for them to succeed. Her endless anxiety began to dissipate, while her confidence that her children knew how to organize their lives increased and reassured her.

She embarked on channeling with great excitement. She had heard many stories about other people's channeling experiences, in which they had succeeded in communicating with certain beings, had received divine enlightenment, and had seen marvelous visions. She performed her channeling experiment absolutely seriously, in an organized channeling group under professional guidance. However, although she did feel wonderfully calm during the channeling - a calmness that she had never known before - to her great disappointment, she did not experience any exciting visions. She was very frustrated, because many members of the group had had the privilege of seeing and hearing astonishingly unique things. The leader of the group consoled her. He explained that the channeling experience varies greatly from one person to the next, and she must not despair.

He explained that she may well be receiving certain kinds of enlightenment, and that certain processes were occurring inside her; she had only to wait patiently until she understood a bit better what was happening. Linda continued doing her exercises. At the same time, she suddenly discovered that topics that had never interested her before, or had seemed alien to her, such as the ecological situation in the world, cruelty to animals and people, and other subjects of this ilk, began to evoke fierce emotions inside her.

While standing on line at the supermarket checkout counter, she noticed some cans of tuna, and suddenly visions flashed into her mind, showing how dolphins, sea turtles, and other rare marine species became trapped in the tuna fishermen's nets, and perished in their exhausting struggle to extricate themselves. Their carcasses were carelessly flung back into the sea. The visions appalled her, and filled her with a sincere feeling of concern for the fate of these wretched creatures that were needlessly abused, just so that someone could accumulate more and more wealth. She discovered a new strength in herself to get up and protest against the injustice.

She saw many visions of this kind in unexpected places and at unexpected times, accompanied by a strong feeling of vocation. She began to relate with great seriousness to global ecological problems, and altered her daily way of life, taking care not to harm the world by her lifestyle and purchasing habits, and raising other people's consciousness to the subject.

At a certain point, she understood that her true vocation lay in concern for the world we live in, and she began to operate in every possible manner to make people aware of the state the world was in, and the bad mistakes that were being made. Gradually, she began to join various ecological organizations, offering them her services as a book-keeper. She cut down her job in her original workplace to part-time, and threw herself more deeply into her true vocation. To her great joy, her whole family became involved in her endeavors, and displayed a great deal of appreciation and respect for their mother's important work. Her eldest daughter, with whom she had always had endless conflicts and rows about her "lack of seriousness and rationality," was her most ardent supporter, joined her mother's struggle, and became her good friend and faithful assistant.

As we can see, the tremendous advantages of channeling can manifest themselves in weird and wonderful ways, helping the channeler to live a fuller and better life, as a result of finding his true vocation, if he so wishes.

* * *

Murray, a retiree of about 65, discovered channeling about two years after the untimely death of his beloved wife. His only son, who lived abroad, was compelled to return home after the traffic accident in which his mother had been injured, and subsequently died, since his father had plunged into a deep depression, and could not function normally on a day-to-day basis. Before his wife's death, Murray had been an active and lively man. After his retirement, he had gotten involved in his hobby - carpentry and furniture-making - and, together with his wife, had enjoyed life and felt great satisfaction with it.

After her death, he lost his zest for life. He withdrew into himself, refused to socialize with friends and acquaintances, quit his carpentry work, and spent entire days in idleness, thinking and speaking ceaselessly about his wife, missing her sorely, and reminiscing about the good days they had spent together. Jeff, his son, watched his father's deterioration with great sorrow. As a result of his constant idleness, Murray's body gradually began to atrophy; he put on weight, neglected his physical well-being and his appearance, and began to suffer from pains in the chest and limbs. Jeff made superhuman efforts to get his father to speak to a psychologist who specialized in loss and bereavement. For a long time, however, Murray refused to hear of it. When he finally did have a few sessions with the psychologist, Murray maintained that it was a waste of time and money, and refused to continue with the treatment. He had been deprived of his entire joy of living, and his heart was filled with bitterness and anger toward life, which had taken his wife away from him, causing him to be a bitter, cantankerous, and self-pitying man.

Murray had always declared himself to be a "rational" person, and had refused to get involved in spiritual matters, since they seemed unrealistic to him. Now he began to search for "heavenly signs" in everything - signs from his beloved wife. The question of whether there really was life after death, and if it was possible to ever meet up with his wife again, in another dimension, tormented him endlessly. It was difficult for him, as a declared skeptic, to accept the possibility of life after death, but on the other hand, he was haunted by a strong feeling that his wife's spirit still existed in some dimension. When Jeff suggested that he join a meditation and channeling group for senior citizens, Murray reacted angrily. However, deep inside, he was burning to know if life really did exist on the other side.

Following a great deal of persuasion, and after the leader of the group, who had a lot of experience working with people of this age-group, offered to come to Murray's house, Murray agreed to give it a try. At first, he was very disappointed that he couldn't begin channeling then and there, and that he had to do the numerous exercises that the group leader gave him every week. Gradually, however, when he felt how the exercises filled him with energy, alleviated his depression, and even improved his state of health (which had deteriorated as a result of his mental state), he began to do the exercises regularly. At a certain point, he even admitted to himself that they gave him a lot of pleasure, peace, and calmness. His obsessive thoughts about his late wife's fate became more infrequent. He began to open up more to his surroundings, and without noticing how it happened, found himself in his workshop once more, little by little returning to his carpentry work.

Hand in hand with his mental recovery, he began to sense the presence of various energies, and, at his advanced age, discovered to his surprise that he was able to see auras. All at once, his life became more interesting, and he understood that, in spite of his great suffering, the world was a wonderful and fascinating place that was constantly renewing itself. The discovery of his ability to perceive auras gave him a new zest for life, and the more he developed this gift, the higher his levels of sight and perception of energies became. These abilities caused him to come out of his shell, go out into the world, look at people, gradually feel and understand their hardships, and experience compassion for them. Little by little, he understood that he should be grateful for what he had, and let go of the pain and the feeling of bereavement that had been a part of him for so long.

When he performed actual channeling, he reached incredible heights. During one of his channeling experiences, he even had the privilege of seeing higher worlds, and had a strong feeling, accompanied by a delicate breeze that he felt physically, that his dead wife's spirit was near him. During his channeling experiences, he even got to see visions from previous incarnations, which helped him understand the course of his life up to that point, as well as the circumstances of his wife's death.

He felt a renewed blossoming, and his life, which was now following a conscious and spiritual course, became full and fascinating. His physical condition also improved, and he began to take care of his body and health, participate in the correct kind of physical activity, and eat suitable, nutritious food. At the same time, his ability to understand people, and feel compassion and empathy toward them developed, and he soon discovered that he was an excellent listener, and could provide a sympathetic ear for many people. Because of his vast life experience, he could help them find solutions to their distress. While he did not feel the need to remarry, he began to join various consciousness groups, and take part in trips and hikes. He made new friends, and his life became full and satisfying. Now it was clear to him that there was life beyond the physical existence of this incarnation, and this knowledge filled him with hope and joy.

* * *

During channeling, the person may well see visions from previous incarnations, especially if he intends and wants to do so. In many cases, these incarnations can provide us with answers pertaining to our present lives. Sometimes, a particular situation for which we cannot find a solution or an answer in any other way, can be solved by understanding an incident that occurred in a previous incarnation, and is responsible for the present situation. It may even concern things that are apparently simple, but disturbing nonetheless. Jessica's story is like that.

From the time she was little, Jessica, a young, nice-looking girl, had suffered from an unidentified disease, which caused the skin of her face to be permanently red and inflamed. There were times when her whole body would be covered with redness, and the inflammation, no less than the disfiguring effect of the disease, caused her a lot of suffering. From the time she was a child, her parents had taken her to see numerous physicians and specialists. She had tried many difficult allergy treatments, but the physicians had ultimately reached the conclusion that her disease was not an allergic reaction.

She spent a fortune on various cosmetics and cosmetic treatments, but nothing helped. The final straw was that she discovered that even cosmetic surgery would not provide a cure for her disease. After she had exhausted every conventional medical option, she began to consult with homeopaths, plant remedy practitioners, and special dieticians. She tried almost every method that could help rehabilitate the state of her skin. While the treatments did in fact help her in many facets of her life, and improved her physical state, the improvement in her skin was negligible.

Her unpleasant state of redness, which looked like a burn or a fungal infection, caused Jessica to withdraw from society and become painfully shy with people. She was a talented musician, and played several instruments with an astonishing virtuosity. But the fear of having to perform in front of an audience, under the glare of spotlights that would emphasize her redness and her hard, rough facial skin, made her fear exposure, and conceal her talent from other people.

She reached the art of channeling mainly because she wanted to learn how to live with her problem, and accept herself as she was. The disease affected every aspect of her life and caused her to suffer from a severe lack of self-confidence and an inferiority complex. She was afraid of establishing relationships with people, for fear of being rejected because of her skin.

After she had spent some time practicing the exercises for meditation, balancing the chakras, and channeling, she began to get involved in channeling. The first few times, she experienced the sensation that she was surrounded by a light of different colors, and feelings of calmness, serenity, confidence, and safety. However, on one occasion, she had an extraordinary experience that constituted a breakthrough in her recovery process.

After performing the first stages of channeling - protecting herself by means of a bubble of color - she linked up with the earth energies and the higher energies, and saw a long path leading through fragrant green bushes to a heavy gate. In her imagination, she opened the gate with a key she was holding. She entered a large, white, airy and pleasant room, which contained her instruments. Soothing, pleasant music could be heard. In her mind's eye, she saw a pool of clear, pure water on the left side of the room. She approached the pool and saw herself bathing in cool, pleasant water, and imagined that the figure of her "inner I" emerged from the water - a kind of white, transparent figure. The figure led her to one of the corners of the room, and instructed her to leave her brain in an opaque box.

When she had done so, the figure indicated the door on the other side of the room. She opened the door. Suddenly, she saw herself looking at an awful scene. She saw a big wooden house surrounded by flames. Although the fire was all around, there were still many possible escape routes. Inside the house, she saw, to her astonishment, the figure of a young woman dressed in a long dress, running panic-stricken among the flames. The flames were devouring her dress, but because of her state of panic, she was unable to escape the blaze.

Shocked, Jessica saw how the fire surrounded the woman. The sight of the fire, which was burning the wretched woman and devouring her body and face, appalled her to the point that she felt that she was unable to continue the channeling. She knew that it was not a good idea to halt the channeling experience abruptly, so in her heart she requested help, and little by little, she watched the scene cloud over. She came out of the channeling experience slowly and carefully, according to the rules. When she opened her eyes, she felt her cheeks flaming and burning, and they were hot to the touch.

After she had calmed down somewhat from the experience, and had done a few grounding exercises, she sat down to think about the vision that had been revealed to her. An intense inner feeling told her that the woman was actually her, in another incarnation. She felt that this was the root of her problem. By a strong intuitive sense, she felt that she had to try to experience the same thing once again, but this time, she had to change the course of events.

And so, a few days later, she requested to undergo the same experience again. This time, when she saw the woman in the burning house, she imagined the woman cool-headedly escaping through a window, and getting out unscathed.

The effect of this "repair" was apparent to Jessica within a short time. Her skin began to lose its redness - gradually, but in an appreciable and obvious way. The inflammation and burning sensation she had always felt also decreased enormously. She continued with her homeopathic treatments in order to strengthen her body and provide it with rehabilitative strength, and she made sure that she ate the kind of food that would provide her skin with all the ingredients necessary for its regeneration.

Now, unlike in the past, when those treatments had not helped in the least, Jessica's skin improved drastically within a few months. Less than a year later, during which time she persisted both in her spiritual work and in her physical treatments, her skin was smooth and pleasant, without a trace of inflammation, and the burning redness on her body and face had disappeared almost totally. Her self-confidence improved by quantum leaps. Within a short time, she began to earn an excellent living in the music world.

Transition to Cosmic Channeling: Channeling with Elements beyond Self-Awareness

Man's simplistic vision sees only up to the horizon, while channeling affords a broad, profound, and virtually limitless vista.

Cosmic channeling extends over the past, over the present, and continues into the future. It is important to stress that coping with the past does not mean its deletion as an obsolete factor, but rather the recognition that the past and its heritage are what caused the person's present existence. Recognition of the past means gratitude to the incarnations of human history in general, and to the whole of personal experience in particular. The crises that man undergoes throughout his life, the wars and disasters that beset society in general - these are the things that raise the consciousness of understanding, love, pity, and compassion, and all the values that derive from human society's past. The elements of the past fertilize man in the present, and accompany him in the future. Man must not be detached from his past. The barriers that imprisoned him in the past, the obsolete moralities, and the social limitations that hampered his individual development, and blocked his personal creativity - all these must be removed. But the past must not be denied, it must not be detached from private and social existence, because it serves as a solid basis for the future.

In view of this, it is possible to understand the cosmic significance of channeling. Channeling permits access to certain realms that everyday life does not. In general, these are things that are concealed in our unconscious; sometimes, however, they are things that have never existed in our consciousness (that is, they are present only in the cosmic existence).

This cosmic awareness is occasionally revealed to us in dreams, and sometimes in extraordinary events that establish a particular truth in front of our very eyes. Although many people think that dreaming is an unconscious experience, at the first moment of waking, the dream is perceived as real and concrete; when it is analyzed, it offers solutions for everyday use. Conscious awareness picks up the connection and interprets it. However, from a broader viewpoint, the dream is not limited to the state of sleep only, and reality (that emerges in the dream) continues before, during, and after sleep and the dream.

Beyond our private world there are superior strata. This is the domain of souls that have departed from the world, superior voices, spiritual guides, or any alien element that expresses its truth through us.

A certain theory claims that every person has a "guardian angel" that guides him through life. In general, this is the soul of a dead person that is helping the mortal, and accompanies him from the day he is born until the day he dies. While he is asleep, it leaves him, but remains within calling distance. This angel does not live our lives, but helps us choose the correct path, and protects us from life's hurts.

In monotheistic religions, it is a superior force, God, that protects each and every one of us, but also allows us free choice.

According to the "guardian angel" theory, the human soul has the power to leave the confines of the body, but the person needs to make prior preparations and take protective measures in order to do this with impunity.

External (cosmic) channeling can occur only after being detached from the time factor and linking up with a different rate of time, while freeing itself from the bonds of the framework of the present. As a substitute for the negative properties, channeling is constructed on love and understanding, belief in personal ability, faith in other people, patience and tolerance, choosing the correct direction in life, seeking the right path, and especially merging with the cosmic rhythm which is beyond the everyday. Channeling takes us to a spiritual world, a perfect world that is based on love, understanding, and forgiveness, which is located on a higher level than that which the channeler reaches when he penetrates his own unconscious, since channeling at this level is the understanding of the nature of the universe, and even more than that, it permits a link-up with cosmic awareness.

This link-up necessitates the destruction of the old conventions, and the construction of a new, impeccable basis that will afford a correct and true view of the existence of the self and of the entire universe. This process is long and exhausting, but its result is liberation from the present-time factor, and the penetration into cosmic time.

In cosmic time, in fact in a future world, awareness is spiritual, and the positive energies rule over the world. They actualize the redemption of humanity, and the era of unconditional love and maximum tolerance, and the acknowledgment of difference, without reference to color, religion, race, or sex.

Conscious awareness will grow out of intellectual honing

and development, and will rise to the highest levels. In addition, with the passage of time, society's tendency to value the good of the individual more highly than the good of society increases. This fact also directs channeling to the individual realm, and while in past years, the trend to interpret social values in a collective way prevailed, the present era emphasizes the value of the individual. This trend will necessitate a higher level of personal responsibility, will place a heavy burden of realizing ambitions on the individual's shoulders, and will further empower strong and dominant individuals.

This is not necessarily a natural tendency, since it is simpler and easier to receive answers from a figure of authority. Self-deliberation is difficult, and decision-making from the standpoint of a high level of personal responsibility is not to be taken lightly.

Channeling via Dreams

Channeling via dreams is an easy and natural way to perform channeling. To tell the truth, most of us spend a lot of our sleeping time dreaming. Sometimes we remember some of the dreams, and sometimes we don't, but whether or not we remember them, our sleep is filled with dreams. The dreams that occur while we are sleeping stem from various sources and play various roles. Some of the dreams involve motifs from our everyday life, which bother us while we are awake. At night, our subconscious releases them so as to relieve the tension that is prevalent during our waking hours.

To the same extent, our dreams are likely to express hidden desires and wishes, as well as repressed fears and memories. But there are additional types and levels of dreaming. Many cases of "telepathic dreams" have been reported: two people, between whom the connection may be very slight, dream a similar or identical dream on the same night; or one person dreams about a particular event that occurred at much the same time as it did with another person. These dreams are relatively common, and are likely to occur in people whose ability to link up to their surroundings, that is, their capacity for spiritual openness and reception, is especially great - consciously or unconsciously.

Various exercises for channeling, meditation and consciousness expansion can increase the ability to dream dreams of this type. An interesting story, told by a friend of mine, occurred while he was working as a section manager of a large factory. One night, he dreamed that one of the workers from another section, with whom he did not have close contact, came out of the door of the building with blood on his hands, and announced that he had killed somebody. The dream shocked my friend somewhat, but he tried not to relate to it too seriously.

The next day at work, during lunch, the very same worker sat down beside him, and in a surprising way - since the two had never held any kind of conversation - told him that he had dreamed the strangest dream the night before. His very sincerity was amazing in itself, but even more incredible was the fact that the worker said that he had dreamed that he had killed his section manager!

Another kind of dream, closer to the matter at hand, is the dream that provides information and enlightenment of various types by means of channeling. These types of dreams are likely to supply answers to questions and problems that are bothering the person, and reveal additional information about various fields that he is involved and interested in. They can even provide him with information that comes directly from other beings. On the highest level, these dreams are called "prophetic dreams."

Many people involved in religion, the arts, and the sciences, have used this type of channeling dream and prophetic dream in their work. Especially famous is the story of Rabbi Jacob of Marvege, one of the greatest French Hassids of the 12th century, who wrote an entire book of questions and answers, in which he would ask questions about Talmudic matters while praying, linking up to the holy names and the names of the angels, and receiving the answers at night in his dreams. Similar to Rabbi Jacob of Marvege, the famous physicist, Albert Einstein, said that some of the equations that he had solved had been revealed to him in dreams; and even Friedrich Kekule, the German scientist who discovered the molecular structure of benzene, did so via a dream in which he saw a snake holding its own tail in its mouth, a vision that led him to make his scientific discovery. Many authors and painters have been helped by scenes and visions that they saw in their dreams, and sometimes they even based entire works on those dreams.

Although dreams of this type are perceived as a kind of "gift" from the forces of the universe, it is also possible to "order" them, when the user's intentions are good and pure. The technique of ordering dreams is relatively simple, but should be done after spending some time practicing the exercises for meditation and balancing the chakras.

You should go to sleep before midnight, but like everything concerning channeling, the technique is flexible, and people who are accustomed to going to sleep later than that can do so. An essential oil burner containing jasmine or frankincense should be placed in the room, to assist in spiritual opening; incense with a light, innocuous fragrance can also be used. The bed should be made up with fresh, clean sheets, and you should shower and put on clean sleepwear.

A very important step that should not be omitted is setting an alarm clock (preferably with a gentle but effective ring) for some time between six and seven o'clock in the morning. A lot of research about dreaming has shown that waking up at that time is very effective in remembering dreams. In addition, it has been shown that massaging the scalp before going to sleep is also helpful for recalling dreams. Put a notebook or a sheet of paper and a pen next to the bed, in order to write down the dream as accurately as possible immediately upon waking. After the preparations, you should get into bed, lie comfortably, and concentrate for some time on the question you want answered by means of channeling - or the problem, the request, the information or the aim of the channeling. (It is very important to keep the thought and the intention as pure as possible.)

After that, massage your scalp gently, using light, circular shampooing movements. Now you must see that your whole body is calm, relaxed and loose. To this end, take deep, slow, calm breaths, contracting the soles of your feet, relaxing them, contracting your calf muscles, relaxing them, and so on, contracting and relaxing your muscles all the way up, until you reach the crown of your head.

Now that all the preparations have been done, you must ask your question, and request an answer. You can turn to the "upper I," or to the universal power of love, to God, or to any other universal force, and ask this force to reveal the solution or answer to you during the night, whether vocally, or by enlightenment - helping you to remember the answer after you wake up, and to make the correct use of it for continued spiritual development and for the benefit of the entire universe.

Now you must imagine a large, golden ball above your head. Take deep, slow and calm breaths, drawing the ball inside you during inhalation, and imagining the golden light spreading through your head, enveloping the pineal gland, and from there flowing to the third eye (between the eyebrows), and going out via the indentation at the base of the head that joins the head to the spinal column. This procedure must be repeated seven times. After doing the breathing exercises, you should sink into sleep, and during this time, the answer to the question should arrive. Sometimes, people experience channeling during the breathing exercises, and the solution to their question is revealed to them. Sometimes, several attempts are necessary, night after night, in order to receive the answer. There are cases in which the channeler wakes up in the morning without any note or memory of the dream, but with a clear knowledge and understanding of his question.

* * *

Glenn moved to a new house with her husband and two small children. For years, she had dreamed of a house with a garden, and now that her dream had come true and she and her husband had managed to buy a lovely house, she felt happy and fortunate. However, about two months after the move, she began to notice many strange occurrences in the house. Various electrical appliances, which had served her well in her previous home, broke down or didn't work properly; there were many cases in which she got a mild electric shock when she touched the appliances, even without operating them; her five-year-old son began to suffer from severe asthma attacks; and regrettable disagreements about small, trivial matters sprang up between her and her husband. Another thing that bothered her was the fact that any plant that she planted in the garden, despite her care in providing it with the most suitable conditions, withered or did not grow. She had a bad feeling that something wasn't quite right in that house.

A friend of hers, who noticed the negative changes that were occurring in Glenn's life, suggested that she try channeling by means of dreaming in order to get to the bottom of these unpleasant events in her life. After Glenn had made several preparations, she went to bed relatively early, making sure not to watch TV for a number of hours prior to that, because she knew that the things she saw on TV had a great influence on her subconscious, and she didn't want them to interfere with her channeling via dreaming.

After showering and putting on fresh pajamas, which

gave her a feeling of purity and cleanliness, she placed an essential oil burner containing frankincense in the room, put clean sheets on the bed, and set the alarm clock for 6:30 am. On her side table, she placed a sheet of paper and a pen so that she could write down the images and enlightenment that would be sent to her during the night. For a few minutes, she concentrated on the question that was bothering her: What was the reason for the incidents, the accidents, and the negative situations that were manifesting themselves in her life and her family's life during the last months, was it connected to their move to the new house, and if so, how could the situation be changed?

When she had concentrated on the question for some time, she massaged her scalp gently, took deep breaths, and relaxed her entire body until she felt that all her organs were loose, calm, and free of tension. Once she felt completely relaxed, calm and serene, she requested God's help in sending her an answer during the night, so that she could help extricate herself and her family from the disturbing situation they had landed in.

After closing her eyes, she began to imagine a ball of golden light above her head, and imagined that she was inhaling it into her head. It filled her whole head, flowed down between her eyebrows, and enveloped the inside of her skull. When she had repeated this procedure seven times, she sank into a deep, relaxed sleep. At a certain point, she dreamed that she saw the house in which she was living, with a man and a woman in it, quarreling violently. She heard the sound of breaking dishes and shouting, and saw vague scenes of deep pain and torment. She had the feeling that the woman who lived in that house had stormed out, cursing the place and its inhabitants.

Glenn woke up with a very bad feeling. She quickly jotted down what she had seen, because the scene was already fading. Although she was shocked and afraid, she discovered that after she had got the facts down on paper, she became calm again, and she fell back into a deep, relaxed sleep until the morning. When she woke up, she rushed to call her friend, to tell her about the dream. Her friend explained to her that the negative energies that occupied the house were still there, and the house and its surroundings had to be purified quickly. She told Glenn that there were many ways to purify the house, but she could repeat the procedure that night, again, and ask for guidance as to the best ways to purify the house of the negative energies that were in it. So Glenn repeated the procedure again, but did not remember any dream or enlightenment. The same thing happened for two more nights.

However, she noticed an increase in her ability to sense intuitively which places in the house and the yard contained stronger concentrations of positive energies. When she explained the situation to her husband, he was relieved to hear that there was an explanation for the unexplained conflicts between them, for his unaccustomed nervousness and unpleasant feeling that he experienced in the house. Glenn did not give up, and continued her attempts at channeling by means of dreams, all the while making the necessary preparations and sincere requests to receive information how to purify her house.

Eventually, one night, she had an amazing dream in which she saw certain corners of the house containing "generators" of transparent quartz (crystals that radiate energy at a high frequency) in various arrangements. When she awoke, she rushed to draw the arrangements of the crystals she had seen in her dream. The next day, she asked her friend to accompany her to a crystal store, where she bought the appropriate number of generators. The very same day, Glenn and her friend placed the crystals in the corners of the house and yard, according to the arrangements that Glenn had seen in her dream.

Within a short time, Glenn and her family felt the energetic changes in the house. Their lives became normal and peaceful once more, her son's asthma attacks became more and more infrequent, and Glenn's good and pleasant relationship with her husband was restored.

Channeling Using Crystals

For many years, crystals have served as a very effective tool for channeling with divine beings, or with the "upper I," for receiving answers, enlightenment, and personal growth and development. Crystals themselves have many exceptional qualities, such as releasing blockages, healing at various levels, prediction of the future, and many other uses. There are many types of crystals, but we will focus on one special type: crystals that contain enlightenment and knowledge inside them.

According to popular belief, there once existed a large continent, called Atlantis. The people of the continent were developed in an extraordinary manner compared to nowadays, and they knew the secrets of the universe and the secrets of the crystals in depth. They developed different methods for harnessing cosmic force by means of crystals, in order to derive benefits for both practical and spiritual purposes.

By means of crystals, the people of Atlantis communicated telepathically with various higher beings, from whom they received knowledge about this and other worlds. The reason why the continent of Atlantis was destroyed was that some of its inhabitants began to use the knowledge and power of the crystals for personal, selfish, and perverted purposes, instead of using them for pure aims, such as peace, love, health and spiritual development.

It is believed that before Atlantis was destroyed, its sages requested that its great wisdom, which was worth more than gold, be preserved, so that it could reach the appropriate people at the right time, many years after the destruction of the continent. However, those same sages knew that if they wrote the knowledge down, or preserved it in any other obvious way, there was the danger that once again, as had happened before, it would fall into the wrong hands, and would be used for selfish or exploitative purposes. For this reason, the sages of Atlantis developed methods for programming the crystals, and for transferring the ancient knowledge to them.

Crystals are tremendously durable, and today there are many of those programmed crystals among us, containing portions of this wondrous knowledge. Of course, there is no clear or obvious way to identify these crystals, or to know what knowledge is contained in each one. This, of course, is so that the right people will link up to the knowledge-containing crystals by themselves, and, by means of spiritual work and channeling, will be able to receive enlightenment and knowledge from the crystals.

These crystals are special, and the only way to discover if they are the ancient crystals in which the unique knowledge was programmed is by working with them. However, in principle, using any crystal, and good, sincere channeling work, it is possible to discover, by linking up to the crystal, many things about ourselves and about the world around us. Crystals can be used for developing the intuition, for effecting mental and physical balance, and even for promoting prophetic dreaming and receiving divine enlightenment. Whoever is attracted to crystals and feels a link to them can use them for expanding his consciousness and increasing his spiritual development, but it must be remembered very clearly that their use is permitted for pure purposes only. If a person uses them for a purpose that is not humane and pure, he risks directing the enormous power that is inherent in the crystal against himself.

In order to begin channeling by means of crystals, the person must first find a crystal to which he links up in an intuitive way. For purposes of channeling, generators of transparent quartz, amethyst, sodalite and smoky quartz are the most highly recommended, but each person must be open enough to sense which crystal suits his particular purposes. By means of spiritual openness and luck, the right person is likely to obtain the crystal that contains knowledge from ancient cultures or that is suitable for channeling with divine beings.

There are also special crystals, called "guiding crystals," and the lucky person who encounters such a crystal will find in it a faithful "guide" for the rest of his spiritual development. This person must understand and know that these crystals, and many crystals in general, have a tendency to move on to another person after they have completed their mission with the first person. This enables them to disseminate their important knowledge to many people. For this reason, the person must understand that the crystal does not belong to him, even if he purchased it, and he must know when to relinquish it. If he tries to hold on to it after it has accomplished its objective, and after he has been given signals to give it up, there is a big chance that the crystal will simply "disappear" in an inexplicable manner, get lost, or somehow find its way to another person.

After you have found the crystal that suits you, with which you feel an intuitive link and an affinity, you must purify it before using it for the first time. To this end, place it in a bowl with sea salt for two to three hours.

(Beforehand, however, you must check that this particular type of crystal cannot be damaged by water or salt, since certain types of crystals should not be placed in these substances.) Afterward, it should be placed on the window sill or in any other place where it will be purified by both sunlight and moonlight. After the purification, you can begin your linking-up and channeling work.

The first method of channeling by means of crystals is simply by placing the crystal under your pillow before going to sleep, and requesting that it relay various messages to you while you sleep. The method of channeling by means of dreams can be used in conjunction with the use of crystals. An amethyst crystal can be placed between the brows, sodalite on the third eye, or a generator of quartz or smoky quartz (or any other stone that your intuitive feeling tells you is suitable) above the crown chakra, with its point facing the crown and its blunt end facing outward. An additional method of channeling is by means of linking up and meditation.

When you link up to the crystal, you must empty yourself of every fear, expectation or prejudice. You must detach yourself from thoughts and emotions, in order to be prepared to receive the knowledge, however surprising it may be, that the crystal wants to transmit to you.

You must begin linking up by meditating for about an hour, during which you cleanse yourself of all personal thoughts and feelings. After meditating, you must lie on your back in a comfortable place, relax your entire body, close your eyes, and place the crystal between your eyebrows, on the third eye. Alternatively, it is possible to sit comfortably, with eyes closed, holding the crystal in your hand, while focusing all your attention on it.

When you achieve a state of total relaxation, you will begin to feel the crystal transmitting gentle vibrations to you. This is the time to ask the question, or request knowledge. You can ask about any problem that is bothering you, request knowledge about various spiritual or practical matters, receive information about the crystal in your hand (what it is used for, what knowledge is contained in it), and many other questions.

You can now either keep your eyes closed, or open them, depending on how you feel, and begin to receive the messages that are being relayed to you. These messages will most likely appear in the form of scenes, visions, various sensations, or as enlightenment and information that reach your brain. You must remain objective throughout the entire channeling process, and not try to divert or change the relayed knowledge. In order to receive an answer to a specific question, it is highly recommended to place a double terminated quartz crystal on the third eye; the answer is likely to come in the form of a scene, or by inner knowledge.

After practicing and gaining skill in channeling by means of crystals, if you want to direct the channeling toward divine beings, it is worthwhile using one of the forms of protection described in this book - a symbol, color or light.

Conclusion

> The meaning of the term "channeling" is in effect bringing the spirit or the soul to physical and actual realization, or in other words, the broadening of the "sensory" world into the subconscious, the unconscious, and the upper worlds of the beyond, with the emphasis on preserving self-expression.

The meaning of the term "channeling" is in effect bringing the spirit or the soul to physical and actual realization, or in other words, the broadening of the "sensory" world into the subconscious, the unconscious, and the upper worlds of the beyond, with the emphasis on preserving self-expression.

As such, the concept is depicted as having tremendous power for the individual. There is no external power that can "break" it, nor any insurmountable barrier that can stand in its path (except for what the individual blocks of his own free will). Success will be attainable in any case.

There is no need to wait for the next world; spirituality will reach this world by creating the suitable framework for its realization. The saying, "The righteous suffer, the wicked thrive," is not necessarily true of the nature of life in this world. When the controlling energies are exploited correctly and by means of appropriate knowledge, they help internalize the spirit of happiness in the human body and its life.

In fact, the theory of crime and punishment and the afterlife changes direction here. Now, at this very moment, the revelation or the enlightenment that everyone is waiting for may well occur.

The unconscious must be brought up to the surface of consciousness, and it will lead to the truth.

Channeling is the stage at which the individual completes himself in every aspect of his being.

Just as a physical injury requires medical treatment, and we do not ignore it, so the soul, mind, and spirit, which are an inextricable part of man's nature, require love, warmth, and attention; suitable treatment will certainly cause the entire body to be healthy, strong, and immune to disease.

The physical body is, in fact, the last layer to be hurt when no attention is paid to the soul or mind. (When it comes to a physical injury, people generally relate to it extremely seriously.) It should be remembered that man was not created to suffer in this world. He was created in order to fulfill himself and live in the happiest and most comfortable way possible.

A person who has self-awareness does not need to be controlled by any authority. Love is the only master that controls him and directs his life. In the absence of love, laws and authority are necessary, but the person who knows how to love himself will never be a victim of other people.

In effect, he will be the "creator" of the reality that surrounds him.

When the power of channeling becomes the preserve of

the public, it will be manifested in art, painting, verbal expression, love, magic, and so on. This is genuine channeling.

As an inseparable part of this process, every person must examine the feelings inside himself, the stimuli and the temptations, and must especially remember all those people whom he hurt intentionally or unwittingly.

The energetic forces in the person must be permitted to lead him to enlightenment, and if it is in his power to help others, he must undertake to perform the task. Then the lost paradise will be realized in this world.